S0-AAF-310

DISCARDED

# Amy Vanderbilt's Everyday Etiquette

# Books by Amy Vanderbilt

AMY VANDERBILT'S NEW COMPLETE BOOK OF ETIQUETTE

AMY VANDERBILT'S EVERYDAY ETIQUETTE

AMY VANDERBILT'S COMPLETE COOKBOOK

# New Revised Edition

# *Amy Vanderbilt's*
# *Everyday Etiquette*

## ANSWERS TO TODAY'S
## ETIQUETTE QUESTIONS

*Drawings by Mary Suzuki and Andrew Warhol*

DOUBLEDAY & COMPANY, INC., GARDEN CITY, N.Y.

THE PUBLIC LIBRARY OF NASHVILLE & DAVIDSON COUNTY

Library of Congress Catalog Card Number 66–12178

Copyright © 1952, 1954, 1956, 1967 by Amy Vanderbilt

All Rights Reserved. Printed in the United States

Ref.
395
V22.1e

*To my sons—Lincoln, Paul, and Stephen John*

67-27257

6762757

This is a question-and-answer book dealing with the problems most frequently presented to the author in her mail, television programs, and lecture appearances. For a fuller and more complete treatment of the complex subject of etiquette, please see AMY VANDERBILT'S NEW COMPLETE BOOK OF ETIQUETTE published by Doubleday & Company, Inc.

# INTRODUCTION

This is a practical, basic etiquette book for today's busy people. It avoids involved discussion of elaborate ritual in favor of answers to specific questions I have received from my readers over the past years. It covers much of what the well-mannered person needs to know about the conduct of his ordinary daily life. There is much here for the managers of small households, for business people, and for the teens.

We are in the midst of a social revolution. Manners are changing but the essential need for manners of some kind remains the same. Good manners are the traffic rules for society in general—not in the purely "social" sense. Without good manners, living would be chaotic, human beings unbearable to each other.

A knowledge of what constitutes good manners makes us comfortable within ourselves and with other people. *Automatic* good manners under difficult circumstances increase our security and our ability to help others achieve social poise, too. Reduced to a phrase, good manners is consideration of other people in respect to their feelings, their safety, their privacy and their full social rights and privileges.

AMY VANDERBILT

*New York, N.Y.*

# CONTENTS

---

# THE SOCIAL GRACES

## Dear Miss Vanderbilt:

### TABLE MANNERS

**Who is served first at table and when is the proper time to begin eating?** F.G.P., Garden City, New York

The hostess is not served first unless she is the only lady at the table or is alone with her husband and children. If Grandmother or even a young girl guest is present, the dishes are first presented to her after inspection by the hostess. When the hostess is serving from in front of her place, with or without the aid of a servant, she is served next to last and her husband last. For her to serve herself earlier will mean her food will be cold and her filled plate in the way.

After several people have been served, guests begin eating so their food will not be cold. And, except at breakfast, the polite husband waits until his wife has been served before beginning to eat.

✓ ✓ ✓

**Is it considered bad manners to take anything to drink to your lips while there is still food in your mouth?** B.C.J., Denver, Colorado

Yes, because this may leave particles of food in the beverage or leave an unattractive smear on the glass. Your mouth should be empty before you take anything to drink. Certainly you should avoid the effect of "washing down" food that is already in your mouth. It is amazing how many people are guilty of this breach of etiquette.

✓     ✓     ✓

**Which is correct—the American way of holding the fork in the right hand, or the Continental custom of holding it in the left?** M.F.P., St. Louis, Missouri

Either is correct, but a combination of the two systems is now often seen and is quite acceptable. Even when one uses the American zigzag method it is sensible to convey cut food to the mouth with the fork in the left hand, with the tines of the fork down. Also, in eating a bit of bread and gravy—by impaling the bread on the fork (in either hand), tines down, and sopping up the gravy—it is now usual to convey the bit to the mouth with the fork tines down rather than up.

✓     ✓     ✓

**How do you get stray bits of food on a plate onto your fork?** O.L., Atlanta, Georgia

A combination of European and American style eating is very usual among sophisticated people and makes it easy for a diner to retrieve skiddy bits of food—like peas—on his plate by using his knife in his left hand as a pusher. But the completely American system is to use a bit of bread as a pusher. One never uses the fingers for this purpose.

✓     ✓     ✓

**Please tell me if it is permissible to "dunk" doughnuts, cookies, etc., either at home or elsewhere.** O.E.C.,Wichita Falls, Texas

Dunking doughnuts or cookies, eating chicken, pie, and other things with your fingers depends very much on the circumstances. If you are having coffee with a friend in the kitchen, dunk if you wish. If doughnuts or cookies are served at a tea, you would be uncomfortable doing so, I am sure. So many of these things depend on good sense and appropriateness. As a general rule I would say don't dunk publicly except under very informal circumstances, and if you dunk, break the doughnut or cookie in half, just as you would break your bread, rather than bite into the whole slice.

✓  ✓  ✓

**Is it proper to tip soup or dessert dishes? And when is soup eaten with a spoon? I sometimes see people drinking bouillon, etc., directly from the cup. Is this correct? E.H., Norwalk, Connecticut**

The tipping of soup or dessert dishes is acceptable if the plate is tipped away from the spoon, not toward the eater. Soup or bouillon served in a handled cup or (Oriental fashion) small, cup-sized bowl may be drunk. If there are vegetables or other garnish floating on top, these may be lifted off with the spoon before the soup is drunk. Noodles or other things which may be in the bottom of the cup are spooned up after the liquid has been drunk.

✓  ✓  ✓

**Does one open one's napkin in the lap as soon as sitting down at table, or is it proper to wait until the food is served? D.O., Macon, Georgia**

Guests wait until the hostess has taken up hers before placing their own, entirely open if they are lunch-size, or in half if they are dinner napkins. Napkins are tucked in only for children. They are never refolded; at the end of the meal they are gathered and laid casually to the left of the place setting.

✓  ✓  ✓

**My husband insists on pouring gravy all over everything on his plate. I feel this is bad table manners. What do you think? Mrs. D.T.A., Butte, Montana**

Gravy—unless it is a gravy in which meat, fish, or other protein is incorporated (rarebits, curries, blanquettes, chilis, etc.)—is never poured or ladled onto rice, noodles, or other than meat on the plate. It is an insult to the cuisine to inundate everything with gravy—or that American favorite, catsup. If you want to eat your potatoes with gravy, dip a forkful into the gravy that has escaped from the meat.

✓  ✓  ✓

When conserves and jellies are served, are they placed on the butter plate or on the dinner plate? U.T.R., Red Hook, New York

These may be served at dinner or lunch with meat and are placed on the side of the plate, as are horse-radish, cranberry sauce, relish, etc. They are incorporated onto the fork as the food is taken into the mouth. Liquid sauces (mint, Worcestershire, etc.) meant for the meat are poured only on it.

ɤ     ɤ     ɤ

What do you do when you discover you have taken some "spoiled" food into your mouth—bravely risk ptomaine and swallow it? Or is it acceptable to spit it calmly into your napkin as though nothing had happened? H.F.B., Nashville, Tennessee

Nothing, not even a bad clam, is ever spit, however surreptitiously, into a napkin. But it is sheer masochism to down, for the sake of manners, something really spoiled. Certainly, a partly chewed mouthful of food looks unappetizing if it has been necessary for you to deposit it from your fork on the side of the plate. It should be screened, if possible, with some celery leaves or a bit of bread. And, in taking it out of your mouth, try not to look as if anything were the matter. After all, if you were eating stewed or canned cherries, you would place the pits in the spoon with which you were eating and place them on the side of your plate without any-one thinking your procedure disgusting.

ɤ     ɤ     ɤ

When you find that you have taken some "foreign matter" into your mouth—gravel, stones, fish bones and such—are they re-moved with the fork with which you have been eating? V.F., Peru, Illinois

No, do not use your fork. Foreign bodies accidentally taken into the mouth are removed with thumb and forefinger, as are fish bones and other tiny bones.

ɤ     ɤ     ɤ

When you have to use your handkerchief at the dinner table, should you excuse yourself and leave the table, or should you excuse yourself and turn your head to use the handkerchief without leaving the table? Mrs. N.J.McC., Concord, Massachusetts

You turn your head slightly, use your handkerchief as quietly as possible, and do not excuse yourself.

✓ ✓ ✓

My husband and I like to make experimental visits to restaurants where foreign foods are served. Is it bad manners for us to order different dishes so that we may taste each other's food? Mrs. C.M., Chicago, Illinois

This is informal but permissible, though only if a fresh fork or spoon is used, with the possessor of the dish then handing the "taste" implement, handle first, to the other person. The other must not reach across the table and eat from a companion's plate, no matter how many years they have been married! If one of the two has had included some item in his order and doesn't wish it, he asks the waiter to serve it to the other, if desired—he doesn't take it on his plate, then re-serve it.

✓ ✓ ✓

I was taught never to reach for anything at the table that wasn't directly in front of me, but this rule seems very much relaxed nowadays. What is your opinion? Mrs. S.C.H., Harrisburg, Pennsylvania

Reaching at table is now preferred to asking neighbors to pass things one can well take up himself, but one should not have to rise out of his seat.

✓ ✓ ✓

Who is in charge of the conversation at dinner, the father or the mother? Is the rule for conversation the same when guests are present as when the family is dining alone? Mrs. B.B., New Hope, Pennsylvania

The mother is always the head of the table and is responsible for the leading of the conversation, whether or not guests are present. At a very long table, when there are guests, the father would lead the conversation at his end. When husband and wife are alone with the family at the table, the husband and wife share the responsibility for the dinner table conversation.

✓    ✓    ✓

**When, if ever, is it permissible to smoke at table?** R.N., Hoboken, New Jersey

Smoking at table is tolerated by some hostesses *at the end* of the meal. Ash trays at the table indicate only that smoking after the dessert course is permissible. It is downright bad manners to go to any dinner table with a lighted cigarette or to smoke during or between courses.

✓    ✓    ✓

**Is it ever proper for a guest to ask for a second helping?** D.G.S., Boise, Idaho

At an informal meal, when he sees that there is plenty of the dish he'd like to have, it is very flattering to the hostess for him to ask for a second helping. However, the hostess should anticipate his request for more. The only reason he might not ask, himself, for another helping would be if there were only one or two more portions on the plate and he knew that there were servants still to partake of the meal. Where food is served from the kitchen, plate style, obviously the guest must wait for the hostess to suggest a second helping, because there may not be more in the kitchen.

At a formal dinner, a guest never asks for a second helping. This is because formal meals have many courses and it is assumed that no guest would want a second helping for this reason.

✓    ✓    ✓

**I see a lot of people doing it, but is it really correct to drink bottled drinks right from the bottle? If so, under what circumstances?** Miss T.S.L., Louisville, Kentucky

This is something like eating a wedge of pie right from the hand. It tastes better and under certain circumstances is quite acceptable. Drinking bottled drinks from the bottle is certainly informal and may be done when people are standing around in a playroom or outdoors at a picnic, at the beach, etc. When they are seated at a properly set table such drinks are poured into glasses or mugs, just as the pie would then be eaten from a dessert plate with a fork.

✓ ✓ ✓

**Can you tell me the proper way to eat bacon—do you always eat it with a fork or can you eat it with your fingers? What about broiled or fried chicken? B.L., Hollywood, California**

I've made a list of some of the foods people do get puzzled about —bacon and broiled or fried chicken are on the list:

## How to Eat Various Foods

ASPARAGUS  Use the fork to reduce the tender part to manageable lengths to be dipped in the sauce. Do not chew up and then discard, however delicately, the tougher ends.

BACON  Very crisp bacon may be eaten in the fingers, but bacon with any vestige of fat must be cut with fork or knife and eaten with the fork.

CAKE  Sticky cake is eaten with a fork. Dry cake, such as pound cake or fruit cake, is broken and eaten in small pieces. Tiny confection cakes (served at wedding receptions, etc.) are eaten in the fingers. Cream puffs, Napoleons, and eclairs, all treacherous as to filling, are eaten with a fork.

CELERY, RADISHES, OLIVES, AND PICKLES  These are taken in the fingers, placed on the side of the plate or on the butter plate (and see "Salt.") Olives, if small and stuffed, are put all at once into the mouth—otherwise they are bitten in large bites and the stone put aside but not cleaned in the mouth.

CHICKEN  (*broiled or fried*)  Chicken must be eaten with knife and fork except at picnics. Bones are not put into the mouth but are stripped with the knife while being held firmly by the fork. Joints are cut if one's knife is sharp enough and it can be done without lifting the elbows from the normal eating position.

CORN ON THE COB  This is only for informal eating and is best eaten on the cob. A long ear may be broken in half, but only a row or so at a time is buttered and seasoned, never the whole ear at once. A mixture of salt and pepper may be made, unnoticeably, on the side of the plate, then spread a little at a time on the corn with a knife as you are eating it. If the corn is to be cut off the cob, the cob is held on one end with the left hand and the kernels cut off a few rows at a time with the dinner knife. The kernels are then seasoned and eaten a forkful at a time, as one eats peas.

FISH     Small fried fish are usually served whole. The head is cut off first, then the fish is held in place with the fork and slit with the tip of the knife from head to tail and laid flat. The backbone is then gently lifted up with the knife and fork and laid on the side of the plate. The balance of the fish is then cut with the fork or knife. Any tiny bones taken into the mouth are taken in thumb and forefinger and are laid on the side of the plate.

FRUITS     *Apples and Pears*     Taken onto the fruit plate and peeled. The sections are then cored and eaten with the fingers or with the fruit fork.

*Apricots, Cherries, Plums*     Eaten in one or two bites, and the stones, cleaned in the mouth, are dropped into the cupped hand and placed on the side of the plate.

*Bananas*     When eaten at the table they are peeled, then broken as needed into small pieces and eaten with the fingers.

*Grapefruit*     Eaten, halved, with a pointed fruit spoon. Sections should be loosened with grapefruit knife before serving.

*Oranges*     Peeled with a sharp knife, pulled apart into segments, and eaten with fingers or fruit fork.

*Stewed or Preserved Fruit*     The pits or cores of cherries, prunes, plums, apples, eaten in compote form with a spoon are dropped into the spoon, then deposited on the side of the plate.

*Watermelon*     If served cubed in a compote, eaten with a spoon; otherwise eaten with a fork. Seeds are dropped into the cupped hand and placed on the side of the plate.

PIZZA     This is usually a finger food. It is folded to make it more manageable. If it is served in a restaurant, it may be eaten with a knife and fork.

POTATOES *Baked* are eaten with a fork, and the skin may be cut up with a knife if one wishes. If the skin is unwanted, the mealy part of the potato is eaten right from the skin with each portion seasoned just before entering the mouth. Except for a child, do not scoop out all the potato, set the skin aside, and mash the contents all at once with butter and seasoning.

*Chips* are eaten in the fingers.

*French Fried* are halved with the fork, if necessary, and eaten with the fork.

*Shoe String* If really dry and impossible to eat with fork, may be eaten with fingers.

SALAD A quarter of iceberg lettuce may be eaten with knife and fork.

SALT If salt is needed for dipping celery or radishes or for corn on the cob it is placed on the edge of the plate, never on the tablecloth. If open salt dishes are used and no salt spoon provided, use a clean knife to take salt from a common container. If individual open salt dishes are at each place, salt may be taken between thumb and forefinger.

SANDWICHES Small tea sandwiches and canapés are taken in the fingers. Double- and triple-decker club sandwiches are eaten at least with the aid of the knife and fork. They may be cut into fourths and eaten in the fingers, or, if too unmanageable, they are eaten with the fork, after being cut into small bits.

SHELLFISH *Clams (steamed)* If the shell is not fully open, take it up and bend it back with the fingers. With the right hand lift out the clam by the neck and dip it first in melted butter or broth, or both alternately, then into the mouth in one bite. Empty shells are placed on butter plate or shell plate, if provided. Do not spoon up remaining liquid in soup plate—it may be sandy—but drink the broth separately provided in the bouillon cup.

*Lobster* (see illustration)

*Oysters and Clams (Half Shell)* Hold the shell steady with left hand and, using oyster fork, lift oyster or clam whole from shell.

Dip in cocktail sauce and eat in one mouthful. Oyster crackers may be dropped whole in sauce, extracted with oyster fork and eaten.

*Shrimp Cocktail* Where shrimps are too large to be eaten in one mouthful, impale them on the seafood fork and bite off a manageable bite. Redip the remaining portion in the sauce, eat the balance. Do not attempt to cut the shrimp in half on the small service plate beneath the cocktail cup as this undoubtedly would be disastrous.

SPAGHETTI  The *aficionado* knows that the only graceful and satisfying way to eat real Italian spaghetti is to eat it with a large soup spoon and a fork. The spoon is placed in the left hand more or less upright in the plate of spaghetti. The right hand uses the fork to separate a few strands and then, with the tip of the prongs against the spoon, to wind the spaghetti into a manageable mouthful. As with any sauced dish, it should be eaten without stirring spaghetti, cheese, and sauce all together, infant style. The timid way to eat spaghetti is to cut it into small bits with the fork and eat it with the fork alone. Thick macaroni is better cut with the fork as one goes along. Remaining sauce of each dish may be eaten with a spoon or sopped up with small bits of bread, which are then eaten with a fork.

TOAST AND HOT BREADS  Toast and the various hot breads— scones, English muffins, Parker House rolls, and so forth—may be buttered whole while they are hot, then broken or cut with the butter knife to be eaten in manageable pieces.

✐    ✐    ✐

HOW TO EAT A LOBSTER—BOILED OR BROILED: 1. Holding the body of the lobster on the plate with the left hand, twist off the claws with the right. Lay on side of plate. 2. Holding the lobster steady on plate, if necessary, lift up tail meat with fork. Cut into manageable segments with knife, dip in melted butter or mayonnaise. 3. Break off small claws and gently suck out meat from severed end. 4. Crack big claws, extract meat with seafood fork or nut pick, dip in melted butter or mayonnaise. 5. With seafood fork, pick out the good meat in the body, including the tamale, the green liver (and in females, the scarlet roe). Real lobster lovers unhinge the back and open the body of the lobster to extract the remaining sweet morsels.

Is it ever correct to have one's elbows on the table when one is eating? I was brought up to think it is not. L.G., Boston, Massachusetts

It is not correct to put one's elbows on the table when one is eating but it is permissible to rest them on the table between courses.

✓   ✓   ✓

I've never known quite what to do about an "accident" at the table. Just recently, while a weekend guest at a friend's home, I inadvertently spilled some jelly at breakfast onto a spanking clean white cloth. I tried to scoop it up with my napkin and managed after a fashion but I wondered later if I had done the right thing. D.E., Riverdale, New York

The best way actually to retrieve a bit of jelly or sauce is to take a knife or fork, scoop up the substance, and place it at the side of your plate. If something is spilled onto your dress or tie, use a clean knife or spoon to get it off and then dip your napkin into your water glass and rub the spot lightly. Everyone has these unfortunate moments, the trick is to carry them off quietly, with a minimum of fuss.

## INTRODUCTIONS

My husband has taken a new job in a different city, and I understand we will have to do a lot of entertaining. For some reason we're occasionally confused and embarrassed about making and acknowledging introductions. For instance, should men always shake hands when they are introduced? What do you actually say when you introduce a man to a woman? Do women shake hands? Mrs. L.B.B., Durham, North Carolina

When men are introduced to each other they shake hands standing, without, if possible, reaching in front of another person. They may smile or at least look pleasant and say nothing as they shake hands, or one may murmur some such usual, courteous phrase as

"It is nice to meet (or know) you." To which the other may reply, "Nice to meet you" or merely "Thank you."

In shaking hands, men remove the right glove if the action isn't too awkward because of the suddenness of the encounter. If they shake hands with the glove on they say, "Please excuse (or forgive) my glove."

Men who meet or are introduced to each other outdoors do not remove their hats unless a lady is present. When a man is introduced to a lady he does not offer his hand unless she makes the move first, as it is quite correct for a lady merely to bow in acknowledgment of an introduction—in fact the usual thing. But of course no lady ever refuses a proffered hand and we should know that European men are taught to take the initiative in handshaking. The words of the introduction between a man and woman go this way: "Mrs. Gardiner, Mr. Longstreth." Or, "Mr. Longstreth, I would like you to meet Mrs. Gardiner." Or, again, and more formally, "Mrs. Gardiner, may I present Mr. Longstreth." Never introduce the woman to the man unless he is a head of state or a head of church, or possibly an elderly and very distinguished man and the woman being introduced is very young. There is much less handshaking in this country, less between women, and women and men, than between men. A hostess, however, always greets all her guests by rising and shaking hands, and all guests should seek to shake the hand of the host and hostess in greeting as well as in farewell.

When women are introduced to each other and one is sitting, the other standing, the one who is seated does not rise unless the standee is her hostess or a much older or very distinguished woman. The rising of one woman for another in this country indicates great deference. It is often a delicate matter to decide whether or not a woman is sufficiently older than oneself to be worthy of the gesture. If not, she may be offended rather than honored. Any young girl in her early teens, however, should rise when introduced to any matron and to any older man of her parents' circle, but she shakes hands only if the older person so indicates. Of course, any woman seeking employment rises when presented to her prospective employer, male or female, and permits the interviewer to make the move to shake hands, or not, as he chooses.

A woman or man introducing husband or wife to another person says, "This is my husband," or "May I introduce you to my wife?" A man's wife would, however, be introduced *to* a much older woman, to a woman of great distinction, or to an elderly and distinguished man, to her husband's boss's wife.

Neither spouse refers to the other socially as "Mr. Brown" or "Mrs. Brown." Nor does a man say "the wife" or "the missus."

No one properly says "Charmed," "Delighted," or "Pleased to meet you" when presented to anyone. In fact, under ordinary circumstances a casual "Hello," or "How do you do?" (to which no answer but a repeated "How do you do?" or a smile is expected) is sufficient. A spontaneous "It's so nice to meet you" or "I am *so* glad you came" or even "I have heard so much about you" is fine when it is really meant—but it is never obligatory. All introductions may be acknowledged with no more than a pleasant glance and a slight bow except those between men, where a handshake is usually expected.

✓    ✓    ✓

**How do a man's bow and a woman's bow differ? Is it ever proper to refuse to return a bow if you're a woman? Mrs. L.G., Port Chester, New York**

A man's bow is a modification of the deep bow he learned as a boy in dancing class. When presented to a lady, he bows first slightly from the waist, eyes on her face, then steps forward awaiting her tendered hand. If she makes no offer to shake his hand, he keeps his own at his side.

A lady's bow is a slight inclination of the head, usually accompanied by a smile. She follows her bow to a man with a handclasp if she wishes. No one properly refuses to return a bow.

✓    ✓    ✓

**When ladies already seated at a luncheon table are introduced to each other, do they shake hands, seated, when they may conveniently do so? Mrs. G.K., Oakland, California**

No, they bow. In this country there is very little shaking hands between women, although the hostess always shakes hands with her guests, male and female, and anyone acting in the role of hostess—say, a teacher at the school, a woman representative of a firm being visited by outsiders—would rise and shake hands with the visitors, women as well as men.

✓ ✓ ✓

**My father, who was a widower, recently remarried. We are very fond of his new wife and wish to know the correct way to introduce her to our children and friends. My sister and I are both married and feel calling her "Mother" is incorrect. However, to say, "My father's wife" seems cold and impersonal. We would appreciate your help. Mrs. L.M., Toledo, Ohio**

Yes, I agree, "My father's wife" is a little cold, especially when such a bond of affection is between you. She is, after all, your stepmother, even though you and your sister are mature. I think it would be nice to introduce her that way. You probably call her by her first name, so you would say, "Molly, our new stepmother, of whom we are all so fond." Something like this would indicate your gracious acceptance of her.

✓ ✓ ✓

**I am a bachelor about to give an important party. Could you tell me how to introduce Mr. and Mrs. Jones to Mr. and Mrs. Smith? Robert K., Cleveland, Ohio**

The simplest way to effect an introduction such as you have described is to say, "Mr. and Mrs. Smith—Mr. and Mrs. Jones." Or, if these are all people you call by their first names and who will presumably call each other by their first names at an intimate party, you would say, "Mary and John, this is Bill and Jean Smith. Bill and Jean, my good friends the Joneses." It is well, as you know, to avoid stiff formal phrases, such as, "Mrs. Smith, may I present Mrs. Jones and her husband, etc." While this is quite correct, it might make for an awkward pause. The simpler way would be better for the sake of the party.

✓ ✓ ✓

**When one approaches a receiving line and is asked to give a name, does one say, "Mrs. Jones" or "Mrs. John Jones" or "Mr. Jones" or "John Jones"? F.F.C., New York, New York**

You just say "Mrs. Jones" or "Mr. Jones." If you are a very special Jones, the person who introduces you finally to the guest of honor sometimes has the opportunity to define you, as it were. The receiving line should never be held up for lengthy conversations, however.

↑    ↑    ↑

Will you please describe the correct procedure for introducing one couple to another (1) when the couples are of approximately the same age, (2) when one couple is older or more distinguished in station than the other? J.L., Alexandria, Virginia

When the couples are about the same age it doesn't matter whose names are mentioned first. When one couple is older or more distinguished—or perhaps guests in your town—you introduce the younger couple to the older one. You say, "Mr. and Mrs. Smith, I'd like to present Mr. and Mrs. Jones." Or if you are to be on a first-name basis, "John and Mary, Bob and Rosemary Hanson," and then to the Hansons, "The Smiths are here from New York" (or some other phrase in which you use the last name of the first couple if you are sure that the second couple does not already know it). You can also tell them the last name when you are on the way over to make the introduction. You can say, "I'd like you to come over and meet the Smiths."

↑    ↑    ↑

At an open house given by a Washington representative and his wife recently there was of course a receiving line, with the hostess first in the line and our representative next to her. As the guests entered I noticed there was some confusion as to who should be greeted first—the hostess or the representative next to her. What is the rule when the host holds such a prominent position? G.M., Washington, District of Columbia

The rule is always the same. One greets first the person first in line, who is the hostess or the acting hostess. Occasionally there is a line made up only of men, and in this case the first man encountered is the one one greets first. As a matter of fact, very often the most important guest, for whom the reception is given, is placed in the middle of the line.

# COURTESIES OF EVERYDAY LIVING

## *The Masculine Graces*

**When a match is used, should a man light his own cigarette first and then his woman companion's? If a lighter is used is this still true? J.C., Lexington, Massachusetts**

A man lights his woman companion's cigarette first. In a high wind he lights his own cigarette first, then he lights his companion's cigarette with his own lighted cigarette if he does not have a lighter or if the lighter does not work in a high wind. In using a lighter he needs merely to hesitate long enough to be sure that the flame is adequate, then he lights his companion's cigarette.

*✓    ✓    ✓*

**Should a man remove his hat to kiss a lady? B.R.J., Bryn Mawr, Pennsylvania**

A man kissing a lady on the street—in greeting or farewell (only) —should always remove his hat, no matter what the weather. He should be careful concerning this courtesy even—or perhaps I should say especially—with his wife or daughter.

*✓    ✓    ✓*

**Do you approve of the custom of men keeping their hats on in the corridors and elevators of public buildings? F.J.L., Brookline, Massachusetts**

Yes—if the elevator is crowded he is more considerate to keep his hat on his head, as holding it in front of him will require more space. If there are only one or two occupants in the elevator— either in a public building or in an apartment house—and there are ladies present, it is certainly courteous for a man to remove his hat.

*✓    ✓    ✓*

My wife tells me that a man accompanying a lady on the street always walks on the curb side. Is this still true when he is walking with two ladies? Does he offer his arm? B.J.M., Skokie, Illinois

In America it is customary for a man to walk on the curb side when accompanying a lady on the street, but the rule is not so hard and fast as it used to be. In Europe the man walks on the woman's left, which may be the inside. When a man is accompanying two ladies he may walk between them, or, conservatively, on the outside, moving to the center position to assist both across the street. He does not offer his arm to a lady, except to an elderly or infirm one, in the daytime, although he does so at night or in bad weather. He offers his arm to assist her across the street but does not propel her by the elbow. He may never take *her* arm except to help her in and out of vehicles, to guide her across the street, etc. In this latter case, incidentally, a woman should bend her arm so that the man may pilot her efficiently.

✓ ✓ ✓

What do you consider the important "don'ts" for a man or boy to remember? E.N.B., Atlanta, Georgia

Do not—
    enter a room before a lady unless it is dark and you wish to make it ready for her
    seat yourself while ladies are standing
    speak or bow to a lady before she has given some sign of recognition
    smoke without asking permission of the lady you are accompanying or sit so near (as in a train) that the smoke might annoy her
    call any but your contemporaries, servants, or children by their first names
    keep your hat on while talking to a lady (unless asked to replace it) or fail to touch your hat or to lift it when necessary
    take a woman's hand, nudge her, or take her arm except to help her up *into* or *out of* vehicles or across the street
    speak intimately of any girl or woman to other men

fail to pull out a lady's chair for her or fail to serve her or to see
that she is served first

speak of repulsive matters at table

criticize another's religion, belittle his race or country, or refer
unnecessarily to his color in his presence

enter any place of worship without removing your hat (if its
removal is expected) and without speaking in reverent tones

laugh at the mistakes or misfortunes of others

fail to give due respect to a clergyman of any faith, to a woman
of any religious order

✦   ✦   ✦

**How should a man refer to his wife to associates, to strangers?
K.B., Richmond, Virginia**

A man refers to his wife as "my wife" to acquaintances, "Betty,"
to close friends, and "Mrs. Green" to strangers. He *never* uses the
phrase *"the* wife."

✦   ✦   ✦

**When a boy takes a girl to a dance in a public place where there
is a checking concession, does he hand her the amount of the
tip that she'll need to get her coat, or should he stand in line with
her, get her coat, then stand in line for his own? Or should she
handle her own coat herself and tip out of her own money?
J.M.W., Jersey City, New Jersey**

Where there are long lines at both checking counters, it is
sensible and courteous for the boy to give the girl the expected tip
and for her to get her own coat while he gets his. At any rate,
they part, and a wise girl has her own tip ready, in case the boy
doesn't think of this extra expense or she doesn't really want him
to assume it. Where no waiting is involved the boy may, of course,
go and get a girl's coat with her, leaving the tip.

✦   ✦   ✦

**I ride a crowded city bus to work every day. I was taught that a
gentleman should stand and give his seat to a lady but most of
the women in the busses I travel seem to be going to work, too.
Why should I give up my seat to them? Is it really considered
necessary these days? J.A., Chicago, Illinois**

I agree with you that businesswomen are used to standing on their own feet. A true gentleman, however, does rise for an elderly woman, for a woman laden with packages or carrying a young child, for a woman who is pregnant or obviously ill. When he does give up his seat he moves at least a few feet away and never attempts to start a conversation. The woman, however, always thanks such a man courteously though briefly for his kindness.

✓   ✓   ✓

**My husband thinks I am difficult because I expect him to wear his coat to the table. He says that a man should be able to do as he pleases in his own home and that wearing a coat at table isn't important. Mrs. J.A.O'R., Nashville, Tennessee**

We have abridged ceremony very much, but a considerate man wears coat and tie (unless he's in a sports shirt) even to his own dinner table. In very hot weather he may ask permission to come coatless, but he should always remember to ask his wife—always his hostess and deserving the respect due one. Marriage is difficult at best, but when it is devoid of expected small courtesies it is intimacy without shock absorbers.

✓   ✓   ✓

**When we go to parties, my husband leaves me almost inside the door and I don't see him for the rest of the evening until it is time go home. It seems to me that this puts the burden of my entertainment too much on the other men present, especially when there is a buffet party. Don't you think that he should pay some attention to me, even though we're married? Mrs. G.N.K., Tulsa, Oklahoma**

Yes, he certainly should. He should not treat you differently than the unmarried girls he took out in his bachelor days. He should see that you have an opportunity for pleasant conversation, that you are given refreshments as needed, and that you are never left too long with what may seem to be an uncongenial companion. His neglect of you at these parties reflects on his own good manners with others.

✓   ✓   ✓

**Yesterday my husband and I went to dinner with another married couple. After we had removed our coats, my husband compli-**

mented the other lady on the dress she was wearing. Since there were only two of us ladies present, don't you think the compliment should have been plural to include my dress? I believe the other lady's husband was embarrassed over it, but no one paid me a like compliment. F.J.R., Denver, Colorado

I think you are begging trouble if you demand compliments from your husband. If you make him feel guilty because he doesn't compliment you when you look nice, whatever compliments he then is able to force out of himself will be meaningless. You must build up a better opinion of yourself. If you have done the best you can about your appearance and you know you look nice, then compliments will come spontaneously. Whether or not they come from your husband is not important because men seem to think that their wives take it for granted that they think them attractive. Sometimes they are reticent about saying nice things just because their wives are their wives. Your husband's comment about your friend's dress may have been spontaneous or it may have just been an effort toward good manners. It did not mean that he thought her dress more attractive than yours or considered her more desirable than you.

✓ ✓ ✓

Every year at Christmas and birthdays my husband gives me an array of personal gifts, none of which ever fits me. Each year I accept them with thanks and later, when possible, exchange them. When I can't exchange them I must give them to somebody else. What should I do? Mrs. J.M.R., Akron, Ohio

Talk the problem over with him nicely, well before Christmas. Say nothing about his previous gifts not having fit you. Tell him you really like his taste in these personal things and how much you look forward to the gifts he is going to select. But give him a list of all your sizes, saying that some of them may have changed. If you find that what he normally selects is unbecoming to you and you have reason to believe that he'd like to be relieved of the need for making these selections, why not tell him specifically what you would like, perhaps hand him an advertisement from the paper or a magazine, marking the size and color you prefer. But in doing this don't exceed what you feel he would normally spend on you on these gift-giving occasions.

⚹ ⚹ ⚹

I have recently become engaged. I notice that my fiancé is becoming rather relaxed about some of the social amenities. For instance, he hesitates just long enough when he stops the car for me to feel that I should open the door and get out myself. Should I make an issue of this now, or should I give in and expect much less manners from him once we are married? Miss V.B., Dallas, Texas

There is no place where manners are more important than in marriage. We should all encourage husbands to maintain the traditional gallantry toward us, not so much for our own sakes but for theirs. It helps a man, I think, to maintain his status at a time when so much—I'm thinking of the independence of women—threatens him. It all seems a little sad if, when a man becomes a fiancé or a husband, he decides to skip the social graces. So encourage your man to be exacting about these courtesies right from the start, for the sake of your man-woman relationship. And of course, too, if he has good manners toward you he will gain the respect of all his associates.

### The Well-mannered Woman

When I call someone on the telephone—a neighbor whom I have never met and who doesn't know me—about some community matter, do I say to her, "This is Ann Little," do I say, "This is Mrs. Little," or do I say, "This is Mrs. John Little"? What if I have met her and we have many friends in common with whom we are on a first-name basis? Mrs. J.L.L., Memphis, Tennessee

In the first instance, you say, "This is Mrs. Little." Then quickly, as she may be confused, "I'm calling for the Emmanuel Church Supper Committee." If you have met several times and you are sure she knows who you are, it would be more friendly to say "This is Ann Little." Then you might follow it with "We met at the Petersons' a few weeks ago." That should place you to her. Don't leave her in the dark, however, if she's to send you a contribution or do something which involves her communicating with you. Be quite clear and say, "May I give you my name and address again. As you may remember, I am Mrs. John Little of Kettle Creek Road." Generally speaking, where the contact is on a very casual and businesslike basis, you announce yourself as "Mrs. Little." Where there is some social element involved you may say "This is Ann Little." However, if you were giving an order to a tradesman, say "This is Mrs. Little of Kettle Creek Road," or, if there would be some possibility of misunderstanding, "This is Mrs. John Little of Kettle Creek Road."

✓     ✓     ✓

**When I was a girl there were certain subjects that could never be mentioned in mixed company. For example, if a woman was going to have a baby, this was not considered a proper drawing room topic. Today things seem to be changed, and all around me I hear subjects discussed and words used that seem very discourteous, to say the least, to the women present. What is your feeling about this? R.L., Helena, Montana**

I feel that in today's society almost any topic in the world is discussible, if there is reason to discuss it and if the discussion of it is conducted with taste and discretion. I know that many men and women of a previous generation find the kind of talk they hear among young people fairly intolerable, and I think young people should take this into consideration and moderate their conversation when older people who might be offended are around. However, the world has changed very much—women have gone into science, politics, the law, into advertising, business, and every other possible kind of endeavor and profession. They cannot continue to expect men's conversation around them to be geared to drawing room levels. The well-bred person does know the difference between vulgarity in conversation and permissiveness of topics discussed. He does not bring up things that have no possible relation to the conversation in progress just for shock effect. On the other hand, tasteful conversationalists have absolutely no compunctions against discussing such things as pregnancy, divorce, separation, political and other scandal, if such discussion is relevant to what is being talked over in the group. Not so very long ago, such things would have been considered very crass as subjects for mixed conversation, especially in a drawing room.

✓ ✓ ✓

What do you think of those meaningless clichés that some people seem to adopt as trademarks? I'm thinking of such gems as "Good-by now," "You can say that again," "like so," and "Out of this world." Don't you think this sort of thing sometimes gets out of hand? K.E., Tucson, Arizona

Yes, I do. Up to a point they can lend a little color to your conversation, but they can easily become second nature, so that you seem to be a person of little imagination, one suffering from a sad poverty of language. These innocuous slang expressions sound particularly inept from a grown man or woman, unless one is using them quite consciously and in fun.

✓ ✓ ✓

We have been meeting a lot of new people since we have come to this community. Some of them put themselves immediately on an easy first-name basis, others seem more reserved. I don't want to seem overfamiliar with those who don't welcome the informality—how do you handle this? Mrs. R.W.N., Lakeville, Ohio

Be slow to use people's first names and try to let the other person take the initiative—as you seem to be doing. A man must never call a woman of his own circle by her first name unless he is asked to do so. If she is willing to be on a more familiar footing, she may call him by his first name without any explanatory preliminaries, but she may say, "Do call me Joan."

✓ ✓ ✓

Recently my husband and I met a very attractive couple at a friend's house. We later invited them to dinner at our house, but didn't invite our host and hostess, for we had entertained them very recently. Later we heard that they were most offended. Were we wrong? S.D., Oklahoma City, Oklahoma

Yes, one should always invite one's host and hostess the first time one entertains a friend first met at their house—or, as a matter of fact, in their company. The invitation must be offered at least, but if it is refused it is then quite correct to entertain the new friend without the others being present.

ヘ      ヘ      ヘ

**I am one of those people who never forget a face but cannot master the art of remembering names. Is there a tactful way of handling a social problem like this?** Miss J.G., Indianapolis, Indiana

If you are warmly greeted by someone whose name you can't recall, say something harmless such as, "Nice to see you" or "You're looking well." Then while looking quite attentive, let the other person do the talking until he or she gives a clue to his identity. Your own expression should always indicate that you remember him well and favorably.

No one is ever pleased if you say, "I know your face—but I can't recall your name." If you have trouble remembering the names that match the faces, always help out the other person who is probably suffering from the same thing. Never say, "Do you remember me?" Instead, in greeting people, identify yourself quickly and gracefully, "How do you do. I'm Joseph Bye." It is more tactful and modest to assume that you are not remembered than to presume that you are.

ヘ      ヘ      ヘ

**How much may a lady make up in public?** I.S., Cleveland, Ohio

Making up in public is much more relaxed of recent years. However, anything too technical in the matter of making up—hair combing, mascara-applying, or application of liquid or cream make-up—are all taboo. A light dusting of powder and an unobtrusive reapplication of lipstick are acceptable—and usual—in a public place.

ヘ      ヘ      ヘ

**I have a friend who seems to have no idea of anyone's privacy. She persists in asking questions about my age, the cost of everything she sees around our house, and she even had the nerve to ask me how much money my husband made last year. I think these things are none of her business, but I don't really want to offend her as I am sure it's just idle curiosity and that she really means no harm. What can I do?** Mrs. E.C.R., Hartford, Connecticut

There are people who seem never to realize that they are offending and who continue their stream of personal questions to the discomfort of all their friends. The safe thing to do in a situation like this is to pretend that no offense was meant—as you say, your friend doesn't really mean to be malicious. If you don't want to advertise your age—and most women don't—you might answer "You know, the women in my family have always been ageless and I like to keep it that way." Women are expected to lie about their age, anyhow, so, even if you told the truth, your interrogator would mentally add another five or ten years. When no tactful answer seems to suffice and the personal probing goes on, the only solution is to be quite frank. Say, without getting angry, "I know you don't realize it, but that is a personal question I don't feel willing to answer." If your friend then takes offense, she deserves to.

*        *        *

I am allergic to cigarette smoke and I get asthma if I am exposed to it. Even sharing an elevator with someone who is smoking starts me coughing.

What bothers me most is that one of the girls at work smokes. She sits near me and must know that it bothers me, but she has never volunteered to go out to the rest room for her hourly cigarette. Also, many of the men who come to see my boss smoke. I would so like to be polite, but when one is allergic this is about as ridiculous as saying that one wants to be polite to a maniac who has his hands in a strangle hold on one's throat. E.C.S., Santa Barbara, California

Your problem is difficult, one hard to work out with the full cooperation of other people—especially those whom you don't know well enough to ask such a favor.

Many allergics find ways to avoid things that bother them without too much social discomfort, or else they have medication they can take when they happen to run into foods or atmospheric conditions that are bothersome. True asthma, however, is another matter, and if the problem is very serious in your case perhaps the only solution will be for you to find employment where smoking is definitely not permitted. Certainly it is impossible to ask those who come to see your employer not to smoke in your presence. I assume that you have seen a competent allergist. In some cases, I understand, psychiatric help is valuable to asthma sufferers.

The important thing, I think, in your case, is not to feel that this is really a matter of etiquette. Many people dislike very much getting into places where the air is blue with smoke. But they do not feel that they can ask other people to cease smoking just because they don't enjoy being surrounded by cigarette smoke. They understand that the adjustment must be on their own part.

✓ ✓ ✓

I have the best next-door neighbor anyone could want. She is always doing something for me and always giving our eight-year-old daughter something. She takes care of my little girl and our dog whenever I have to go shopping or see the doctor. She does all this without pay, which would make her mad if I offered it. Should I get her a gift all her family can enjoy? Or what can I do to show my appreciation? Mrs. H.E., Fresno, California

Your neighbor gives her services to you with loving affection. There must be many talents that you have that could serve to return her many kindnesses. If you are a good cook and she has a freezer, perhaps when you are baking a pie you can bake one for her, either for her freezer or for immediate use. If you have a way with flowers, perhaps you can make her a flower arrangement and give it to her, together with the container. If you sew well, perhaps she would enjoy a pretty apron or some potholders for her kitchen. If she is alone at night, you could invite her to your house for dinner or take her to the movies. I wouldn't wait for Christmas to return these kindnesses, but I'd try to do little things for her from time to time that will show how much you appreciate what she does for you.

✓ ✓ ✓

What is the proper procedure to follow when people insist that you visit at their home but will not accept an invitation to visit your home, no matter how many times it may be presented to them? I have a friend who always wants me to "come over," but when I ask her to spend an afternoon with me she will reply, "Why don't you come over here?" I don't feel I should say "I invited you first," but believe me, sometimes that is exactly what I think I should say. Mrs. J.B.J., Detroit, Michigan

Some women are so housebound, so domesticated, that they lose track of the fact that in going out of their homes into those of their friends, instead of expecting everyone to come to see them, they are extending a real courtesy. In a case like this, this woman does seem to imply that she thinks her home is the one which, for some reason or other, is preferable for entertainment. No guest is comfortable being a perpetual guest. We should all be permitted to reciprocate as we can for entertainment received. It does not have to be on the same level at all. This writer would be quite justified in saying sometime to this thoughtless friend, "I invited you first." If she still refuses to come, there is something very wrong in this relationship.

✓     ✓     ✓

What can I do about my mother-in-law prying into our private life? She is a country woman and has no desire to learn about city life and cleanliness. When I take my two small children to her, her house is never clean, and when my husband wants to see his boyhood friends, she tags along. We are building a house of our own, and she even criticizes the fact that we want a fireplace, saying that it is "old-timey." I can't put up with this much longer, but I certainly don't want to have a fuss with her. I have just stopped going to see her. Mrs. R.L., Mesquite, Texas

It is hard for a mother to stop making suggestions just because her son has married. But if you can take these suggestions in good spirit and do just as you were planning to do anyhow, in time she may understand that it is you and your husband who must make the decisions about such things as whether or not you will have a fireplace in your house. I would not worry about whether or not her house is clean when your children visit her, as the important thing to them is the love and affection she shows them. So try not to project your feeling of criticism toward your mother-in-law to the children. They need to love and respect their grandmother, even if her ways are different from yours. In time, when she sees how comfortable you are and how attractive cleanliness and neatness are, she may try to imitate your way of living and even ask for your advice. Try to respect her as the individual she is and with the limitations she has. After all, the background she created produced your husband, whom you undoubtedly love very much.

✓ ✓ ✓

Now that my children are older, I am able to hold an afternoon job at the office where I used to work. My friends all know that I have quite a problem getting through my housework in the morning in order to do this. But one or two of the girls who haven't as much to do as I have will get on the phone when they know I'm home, and it seems to me that I just can't get rid of them without being rude. How can I handle this and still keep them as friends, because I do like them? Mrs. A.S., Houston, Texas

Your friends have a social need for you, or they wouldn't call at such length. But your friendship will suffer if you don't deal honestly with the difficulty. Say something like this: "I'm so glad to hear from you, but you know I'm rushing to get through so I can get to work. May I call you tonight?" If this doesn't work just say: "Really, I can't talk now. I must finish up. I'll call you back just as soon as I can" . . . and hang up! If this is said in a properly reluctant tone of voice, no intelligent person can be offended—at least not after she thinks it over a little. As for you, you have no choice. Your home and your work must come first.

✓ ✓ ✓

When one person makes the telephone call, shouldn't she be the one to terminate it, not the one who's being called? Mrs. P.E.J., Port Richmond, New York

It's not too important, really. But usually it's the other way around. The one being called makes the necessary response, then, never too abruptly, hangs up.

✓ ✓ ✓

Since childhood I have been taught to say "Yes, sir" and "Yes, ma'am" to my elders. Recently in a family discussion, several members of my husband's family told me this is incorrect, that it should

be simply "Yes" or "No," with no exceptions to age or position.
B.D.W., Charlotte, North Carolina

Usually when one has achieved adulthood he drops the habit of
saying "Yes, ma'am" and "Yes, sir," unless he is a domestic. We
think it is more democratic to say, even to one's employer, "Yes,
Mr. Adams" or "No, Miss Jones." However, "Sir" and "Ma'am"
are still very common in the South. Younger men use the "Sir" to
older ones and often younger women may say "Ma'am" to older
women, without loss of social prestige. Perhaps your husband's
relatives are from the North where this is a less common custom.
If saying "Yes, sir" and "Yes, ma'am" to older or more distinguished people seems natural to you, I see no reason why you
should change.

✦   ✦   ✦

Does the fact that you have a "green thumb" and love to work in
the garden and take care of the lawn have any reflection whatso-
ever on your not being a refined person? I love the outdoors and
plant shrubbery, trees, flowers, and maintain my entire lawn. Recently a neighbor remarked that this was rather unladylike. Is it?
H.P., Miami, Florida

Certainly not. It is a wonderful, creative hobby. Just join your
local garden club, and you will see how many other "unladylike"
ladies there are.

✦   ✦   ✦

Is it proper for a single girl to have dinner in a bachelor's apartment without a chaperone? F.S., Bangor, Maine

Social conventions can do very little to protect a girl really bent on
getting into difficulties. In this case, a girl not out of her teens
would do better to avoid such a dinner engagement unless others,
considerably more mature than she, are present. Perhaps a good
yardstick for her would be "Could I tell my mother where I am?"
A career girl, from her twenties onward, can accept such an invitation but should not stay beyond ten or ten-thirty. If others are
present, she might stay as late as midnight but not beyond. An old
rule and a good one is, "Avoid the appearance of evil." It is still

very true that men value little those girls who have no strong sense of propriety themselves.

✓   ✓   ✓

By mutual agreement I stopped dating a fellow about six months ago, after going with him for eighteen months. Along with smaller gifts, I received a watch and a portable radio from him. I have been trying to decide what I should do about returning them. I know he probably won't accept them now, but I feel I should make the offer, although I don't want to offend him. Miss D.S., Toledo, Ohio

You shouldn't, you now understand, have accepted these expensive gifts in the first place. Then, without offending him, you could have said, "This is very kind of you, but I really can't accept such an expensive gift." Now the only thing to do is either to speak to him or write to him and say that you feel you really should not have accepted these gifts and that you would like to return them, although you want, of course, to remain good friends. He probably won't want them back, but at least you will know that you have made the proper gesture. And in the future, never put yourself in a position where a man can say, should a relationship break up in a less friendly fashion than this one did, "She was willing enough to take all kinds of expensive things from me, but when she got tired of me, that was that." Friendship between a man and a woman should be voluntary, not obligatory because of too many favors and gifts accepted. You must always feel yourself free in such a situation until and unless you have given your promise of marriage.

✓   ✓   ✓

There is a single man in my office whom I like very much and who has been nice to me but who hasn't asked me for a date. I live with my parents. Would it be all right to ask him to come and see me? A.M.M., Flint, Michigan

Yes, if you are rather casual about it and invite him first when there will be others of your age present. If he refuses your first invitation with obvious reluctance you may, after a discreet lapse of time, try again. If again he refuses, do not offer him a third invitation. However, by this time he may be sufficiently interested to offer you an invitation of his own. While you should never be overly aggressive in the pursuit of the male, you should realize that a man is more inclined toward a woman who shows obvious interest in him than toward one who seems completely indifferent. While many a man yearns desperately for the unattainable, he most often settles in time for girls who make him feel attractive and desirable, so long as there is no hint of desperation in their approach.

✓  ✓  ✓

**I make a good salary, more than most of the men I go with do. I like to go to the theater but get tired of going "Dutch" with girl friends. Could I get seats and ask a boy? E.H., Greens Farms, Connecticut**

Yes, but don't repeatedly ask the same one to go to the theater with you when you are buying the tickets. Here again, be very casual in your invitation. Say, "I have two tickets for ———— next Saturday night. Would you like to go with me?" He will then understand he is not expected to pay for the tickets. If he accepts, however, he is responsible for your transportation to and from the theater and for any entertainment of you, before or after, he feels able to manage. Give him the tickets when he picks you up and avoid in every way seeming to be in charge of the evening. If you feel self-conscious about having had to furnish the tickets, it may help you to know that not so many generations ago it was considered ill-bred for a young lady to accept any such entertainment from a man—her parents or servants always made such arrangements or reimbursed him for anything of the kind. It has always been quite correct for a girl to invite a man to the theater, a concert, or the opera with the tickets presumably furnished by her parents.

✓  ✓  ✓

**How and when is it ever "proper" to invite a doctor to our home? Mrs. M.M., Baton Rouge, Louisiana**

This is a delicate matter. I assume you mean your own doctor. If, on your visits to him, you find that he himself engages you in some social conversation each time and seems anxious to prolong the visit for this reason, it is a quite proper thing to feel him out, as it were, to see if he would be interested in a social invitation. You might say, "Doctor, my husband and I hope that you and your wife will have time to come to our next cocktail party (or dinner party, whichever it may be)." If the doctor really feels that he has time—and interest—to pursue the matter, he will say, "I'm sure we'd love it. Just let us know." If he says something like this, "Well, that's very kind of you, but we have so little time for social activities," you will know that it is probably impossible for him to expand his limited social life and that this is no reflection on his feeling for you. Certainly, if he is married, you do not exclude his wife in invitations, and the invitation, when it actually is sent or given over the phone, should be directed to her.

*       *       *

**I am a doctor's wife. My husband's patients load him with all kinds of gifts, often extravagant ones, at Christmas. We wish they wouldn't. Mrs. R.S.S., Detroit, Michigan**

Our doctors at Christmas receive a great many presents from what they call "G.P.'s" (Grateful Patients) when in too many cases, I'm afraid, they'd much rather have their bills paid with greater promptness. People do feel a warmth and gratitude to their doctors and often feel impelled to give them gifts. Doctors themselves tell me that often they would prefer a little more restraint in the matter, especially where there is actually no social contact between patient and doctor.

*       *       *

**I had an argument with my girl friend about whether you should tell a strange woman you see that her slip's showing or that she has a run in her stocking. I always do, but my friend says it's none of my business. Am I right? A.M.W., Montclair, New Jersey**

This is a delicate matter. A woman who looks friendly and relaxed may welcome your calling such a thing to her attention if you can do it privately and casually so as not to embarrass her before others. The tactful time to tell a woman such a thing is when she's some place where she can do something about it, such as a dressing room where she is repairing her make-up and is obviously unaware that her costume needs attention, too.

## INTERFAITH MANNERS

**I am not a Catholic, but when I pass a Catholic church with my friend he tips his hat because he is a Catholic. What should I do? Mr. R.O'M., Tampa, Florida**

Give your friend's church, when you are in his company, the same deference as you would give his mother, should you encounter her on the street. Raise your hat, too, out of courtesy to your friend's reverence. The same rule holds true if you should encounter a priest while in his company. Your gesture is social, only.

*✓      ✓      ✓*

**I have some friends who are Conservative Jews. They do not eat ham or seafood. Does this mean that if I have a buffet dinner I may not have either of these foods on the buffet if my friends are present? R.C.C., Pittsburgh, Pennsylvania**

No, you may place these foods on a buffet, but you let your Conservative Jewish friends serve themselves from the buffet. They will avoid the ham and seafood. Do not attempt to serve them a filled plate that has either of these foods on it, as they then would not properly eat any of the foods with which the seafood or ham had come in contact.

*✓      ✓      ✓*

**Now that the rules for Catholics have been changed concerning the Friday fast, what days do I have to consider when entertaining them? And must I serve fish on those special days? Mrs. F.D.V., Hershey, Pennsylvania**

Catholics abstain from meat now on Good Friday, Ash Wednesday, and all Fridays in Lent. When you entertain them on these days you don't necessarily serve fish. Any non-meat dish will do. If you have a buffet supper, just be sure there are dishes that Catholics may eat and they will make their own selection.

*✓      ✓      ✓*

**I have a friend who is a very strict Methodist. When he visits us, is it incorrect for us to serve wine at the table?** Mrs. W.L.J., Memphis, Tennessee

You may serve it, but when it is passed he, of course, will refuse it. He cannot be offended at your following your usual custom.

✓ ✓ ✓

**I am a clergyman. I am expected to make regular pastoral calls upon my congregation, but as I live in a simple, suburban community where there are few servants, I find that my call, no matter what time of day I seem to pick, interferes with the routine of young mothers. Do you think I should phone before calling?** Dr. J.W.M., Montclair, New Jersey

Yes, I do. The clergyman's call is one that should be received in dignity. It is very hard for a young mother with a household and children to cope with to find that she is opening the door, even in the early afternoon, to her clergyman when she is not prepared to receive him. If she has some forewarning of his visit, she can perhaps arrange to be free at that time and to enjoy the spiritual aspect of such an occasion without interruption.

✓ ✓ ✓

**When I make up my list of friends to whom I am going to send Christmas cards, I never know whether or not to omit the names of Jewish friends. What is proper?** N.A.D., Portland, Oregon

It depends, I think, on whether your friends are deeply religious Orthodox Jews or perhaps those who think of Christmas only as a gift-giving holiday and celebrate it as such especially if they have children. It is, perhaps, better to avoid cards illustrating the Nativity if you desire to keep your Jewish friends on your Christmas card list. Many Jews themselves now send non-religious Christmas greeting cards, have Christmas trees, and give and receive Christmas gifts.

✓ ✓ ✓

**I like the idea of bright and amusing Christmas cards, but I notice that they are increasing in number every year. However, I notice**

that most of my Catholic friends send me religious cards, and I wonder if there is any rule about it. L.A.O., Fort Worth, Texas

No rule, really, but many Catholics are offended by the increasing commercialism of Christmas and by flippant Christmas cards, some of which are really in bad taste, no matter what your religious belief.

*    *    *

Is it proper, when attending Church, Catholic or Protestant, for a single girl or even a married woman to give a donation or offering when she is with her escort or husband? Or should she refrain from doing so and just let her partner contribute? A.M., Cresson, Texas

The church service is not a social occasion. Therefore I would say that a single girl escorted by a young man makes her own donation to her church or to a church they are visiting. Where a woman is accompanied by her husband he would make the donation or offering for both, as head of the household.

# ENTERTAINING

## *Dear Miss Vanderbilt:*

### HOSTS

**When a group of ladies meet at a home, is it proper for the hostess to smoke a cigarette and not offer one to her guests? Or should she not smoke when no one else does? J.B., New Orleans, Louisiana**

She should offer cigarettes to her guests, and, if they refuse, then I hope she will at least limit her own smoking. It would be courteous of her to ask the others if they mind if she smokes—just as a man would. Of course, if someone does mind, she should not smoke.

*1    1    1*

**How many drinks should the hostess figure per person at a cocktail party, and what are appropriate drinks to offer? M.P.M., Boston, Massachusetts**

It is usual to figure three drinks per person for a cocktail party. Some guests will take one drink, some none, and some three or four, but it works out to an average of three. Most-liked drinks are martinis, manhattans, scotch, rye, or bourbon, with the usual mixers. It is often possible to arrange to have unused bottles returned to a hotel bar or to a liquor store furnishing the supplies.

*1    1    1*

When friends and guests come to your home to spend the evening watching television or playing cards, is it expected of the host or hostess to serve refreshments? B.C.B., Columbus, Ohio

It is usual to offer something informally, so long as the serving of these things doesn't interrupt the viewing or the card playing. On certain occasions a late supper is served.

*      *      *

An older relative of ours visits us occasionally from another state. Naturally she pays her transportation here. We have planned a vacation trip to take this relative along in our car. Is it sufficient for us to pay the car expense and for the relative to pay her share of the food and lodging? Or, since she has spent money to come and visit us, are we supposed to pay all expenses of the trip? F.J.O., Carlsbad, New Mexico

In matters such as these, one needs to be frank. It seems unlikely that a couple such as yourselves should be expected to do more than pay the car expenses in such an event. But you should give your relative a chance to accept the invitation under these circumstances or return home before you make the trip.

*      *      *

Sometimes, when we entertain, some guests bring us gifts more or less for the house. I never know whether to open them in front of the others, put them aside with murmured thanks, or just what. Mrs. M.V., South Ozone Park, New York

As "house gifts" are purely a matter of volition on the part of guests and are not really expected, the hostess does not open them ostentatiously if other guests who have come empty-handed are present. She thanks the donor quietly, puts aside the gift, and later privately opens it. She then thanks the giver in a way that makes him understand that she knows what she has been given and appreciates his thoughtfulness. In a party where one guest is from quite a distance and the others are all local people who see the hostess constantly, it would, of course, be perfectly suitable for the out-of-town guest who has come with a gift to enjoy seeing the hostess open it in front of the others. This is a matter for discretion.

And certainly one cannot ask small children not to open the gifts guests bring. The important point is that guests sometimes bring gifts and sometimes they don't. Those who don't should not be embarrassed by those who do, when the occasion is not definitely a gift-giving one or even if it is.

✓     ✓     ✓

**My husband occasionally receives an invitation for both of us. He frequently is puzzled about how to handle this gracefully. What should he do?** Mrs. L.S.S., Green Bay, Wisconsin

When your husband does receive an invitation for you both, he must always say something such as, "I'll have Helen call you about this," or, if it is a telephone call, "Will you speak to Helen?" This is not only a courtesy to the wife, but it prevents confusion in the matter of invitations. Whenever a couple is entertaining together, it is the wife who issues invitations and accepts them. She is, in effect, the family's social secretary.

✓     ✓     ✓

**The husband of a woman we like very much often drinks too much at parties, then tells off-color stories that embarrass everyone present. We hate to cut them off our list because we like her so much. What can we do?** Mrs. K.N., Coral Gables, Florida

Cease inviting them to parties. Entertain them alone and close the bar after one drink has been offered before dinner. Serve the meal promptly without wine. Do not offer after-dinner drinks. Choose a week night to entertain them. If the husband tells an unacceptable story, look blank and let a pause occur in the conversation.

✓     ✓     ✓

**When guests are leaving, is it correct for the host or hostess to open the door for them or should the host (or hostess) allow the guests to open the door themselves?** Mrs. H.B., Farmingdale, New York

You must be sure to let the guests make the first move toward going home. Then, once they have taken the step, you may indeed lead the way to the door and open it for them. If there is a host, he performs this function, unless at a large party he is occupied with other guests and has perhaps said good-by to the departing ones in the living room. In this case the hostess may bid them good night and open the door, or she may bid them good night in the living room and another member of the family may see the guests to the door or a servant may do so. In some instances where guests are very well known to the family and must leave early, they make their adieus very inconspicuously and often let themselves out.

✓ ✓ ✓

So often when I invite people in to dinner they break up into little groups after dinner and tend to stay in them until the party is over. How can I, as hostess, get people to move about and meet each other? Mrs. A.J.O'C., Winston-Salem, North Carolina

As hostess you watch just such situations as these. If within small groups there is obvious congeniality, it is not necessary to break them up, but you can introduce from time to time other members into the group to keep it fluid. And perhaps from time to time you may remove a member from the group who doesn't seem to be partaking too enthusiastically in the conversation. He might enjoy another group better. One pleasant device toward the end of the evening is to try to bring all of the groups together in a general conversational circle. If this is done at some time, it doesn't really matter too much if much of the conversation has been in individual groups.

✓ ✓ ✓

Our apartment is furnished in Early American pieces, many of which we refinished before our marriage. It was very hard work but gave us a great deal of pleasure. Now that we are married we entertain at least once a week and usually serve in the dining room. Time and again one or two persons out of a group make themselves exceedingly comfortable by placing their heels on the rungs of our ladder-back chairs and twisting their feet up and down while carrying on a conversation. I agree with my husband that this is very rude and inconsiderate, but I would rather not say anything about this to my guests, as I feel it might put a damper on the party as well as on my spirits. He, however, speaks right out and tells them to please remove their feet from the furniture. Can you tell us the most tactful way to handle the situation without embarrassing anyone? I enjoy their company, but my husband refuses to invite these certain people once he sees how they act. Mrs. L.R.J., Orange, New Jersey

I remember a woman who was made absolutely miserable by her husband's friends. She loathed their relaxed manners and ran around after them, emptying ash trays even before they were filled, asking them to take their feet off the coffee table, putting coasters under their drinks, etc. Needless to say, she did not reform her husband's friends, but she did alienate her husband. And the friends eventually refused to come to the house. The moral is here: Either you accept, within reason, the manners of your friends, or you make new friends whose ideas of decorum concur with your own.

✓　✓　✓

I have guests who put their cigarettes out in my coffee cups. What can I do? Mrs. S.C.H., Los Angeles, California

Very firmly place an ash tray within reach and say, "Would you mind using this, please."

✓　✓　✓

We have moved into a new house. Our friends all are anxious to see it, and we like to show it off. I have been having a series of informal dinners for them. As I have no maid and the dinner preparation requires all of my attention, how can I courteously suggest that guests refrain from prowling about on their own until I can be with them? It is impossible for my husband or myself to show each guest around individually, and we'd like to do it together when all are assembled—and after the dinner hour is over. Mrs. S.C., Allentown, Pennsylvania

Simply say, "I know that you will want to see the house, but let's have dinner first and I'll show it to you later, all together. I think it will be more fun that way."

✓　✓　✓

My children go to public school. I find that it is more or less expected that sometime during the term the teacher is invited to visit the homes of the children in her class. Sometimes she is invited to tea or sometimes to dinner. Would it be all right to ask a teacher like this to a party? T.J., Terre Haute, Indiana

No, not unless you know her well socially. Visiting the parents of a child is part of a teacher's work, although a voluntary part. She is often invited to dinner, but she goes to get to know the parents better in relation to their child. She couldn't very well accomplish this mission if she were invited to a general party.

✔ ✔ ✔

I would like to know the proper approach to a friend who insists upon blotting her lips on my best linen napkins when she is dining at my house. This leaves a large lipstick imprint. What can I do about it? F.C.R., Austin, Minnesota

Lipstick marks are inevitable on linen napkins, but for a guest to deliberately blot her lips on a linen napkin is thoughtless, to say the least. The lips should not be rubbed with a napkin, they should be gently dabbed. Nevertheless, the napkin will gather lipstick traces. Your solution is either to use large-size dinner napkins in paper (many of which are very attractive these days) or to go over the napkins immediately after the table has been cleared and put some lipstick remover on the soiled napkin so as to loosen the stain before the napkins are laundered. I don't see how you can speak to your friend about this habit without offending her, unless some day you just happen to bring up the subject of the difficulty of getting lipstick out of napkins and ask her what method she uses. Perhaps she'll take the hint.

✔ ✔ ✔

Will you please say something about the preposterous incorrectness of a host and hostess collecting a fee from their guests to help defray the cost of the party to which the guests were invited? This recently happened to us, upon our arrival at an open-house party celebrating moving into a new home. Nothing had been said at the time the invitation was extended to indicate that it would be required of each guest to contribute for food and drinks. It seems to me that no one should be expected to have a party that will topple his budget, but if one cannot afford to extend ordinary hospitality without collecting a substantial fee from each guest—enough to buy a good dinner at a restaurant—it can't be feasible that the party is essential. When will some people learn? Mrs. J.R.C., Oak Park, Illinois

I can't imagine this myself. I can imagine that among quite young married couples, at a co-operative party, people might be asked to bring their own drinks and food. Everyone knows everyone well and understands the financial situation. But for someone to invite people such as yourselves and not mention that a fee is going to be charged at a private home is, I agree, indefensible. Better a party with hot dogs and coffee than one like this.

✓   ✓   ✓

We are going to give a large "at home" without outside help. We are three boys in our late teens, but the party is also for the friends of my mother and father. My question is, "Who should open the door for guests and who should welcome the guests?" P.R., Decatur, Illinois

Any one of you boys or your father may open the door as guests approach. Your mother stays in the living room, rises and greets each guest as he approaches. The hostess always rises to greet any guest, male or female, and extends her hand. At the end of the afternoon or evening, whichever it is, you and your brothers and father will help the guests into their coats and show them to the door after they bid your mother good-by in the living room. As the party tapers off, of course, she may wish to approach the door to say good-by to several at a time. If taxis are needed, one of you boys or your father will summon the cabs or see unescorted ladies into their cars.

# GUESTS

Is it proper to smoke a pipe of any kind at a formal dinner when cigarettes and cigars are passed? C.J., Mason City, Iowa

Yes, if one of the new, small dress pipes is used and if the tobacco is mild. Even then, it is always polite to ask the hostess if she minds a pipe.

✓          ✓          ✓

At a formal dinner, must the men and women separate when coffee is served as they used to in Victorian times and still do in England, the ladies having their coffee together and the gentlemen remaining at the table? T.A.A., Bakersfield, California

In this country we usually have our coffee together, either in the dining room, living room, or library.

✓          ✓          ✓

When a guest enters the room at a party, whom does he or she greet first? T.K.W., Newark, New Jersey

The hostess, then the host, then the guests. The host and hostess always rise when a guest approaches for this traditional greeting.

✓          ✓          ✓

The dinner party is in progress, and one guest comes late. Must all the men rise for introductions? P.L., Memphis, Tennessee

No. In the case of a woman guest she slips quickly into her seat indicated by the hostess after brief greeting, and the man to her right, alone, rises and seats her. The hostess does not rise because then all the men would have to rise with her.

✓          ✓          ✓

If I am an overnight guest in a house where there is no maid, should I strip the bed in the morning before leaving or leave it as it is? S.F.P., Brooklyn, New York

Ask your hostess which she prefers. If you are a good bedmaker and have the time, you might ask her for clean sheets and make up the bed yourself in order to save her work.

✓          ✓          ✓

My wife and I and my sister were informally at a friend's house the other evening. Our host and hostess were a married couple without servants. During the evening, in the living room, the hostess brought in coffee and ice cream. My sister says that I should have gotten to my feet as my hostess approached my chair and taken from her hand the cup of coffee and ice cream. I have argued that this is not necessary and that I was not discourteous and did not show bad form when I remained seated. Who is right? D.E.C., Augusta, Georgia

Your sister. As soon as the hostess had finished apportioning out the ice cream and coffee, you should have risen and assisted her in passing it to the guests.

                    ✓      ✓      ✓

The other evening my husband and I had to have dinner with some very important clients of his. The client and his wife proceeded to drink entirely too much and were obviously intoxicated in the restaurant in which we were eating. I was afraid that if we sat it out through all the courses of the dinner, some episode would occur that would make it impossible for my husband to have proper relations with them again. So after the meat course I suggested that we skip dessert and just have coffee before leaving. My husband felt that perhaps I was rude. Do you think so? C.N., Albuquerque, New Mexico

No, I think you did the right thing. You undoubtedly saved a very difficult situation. If the client and his wife had made a serious disturbance in the restaurant, they would have somehow blamed your husband and you for it, and your husband might not have been able to go on with his business relations. Your tactful maneuver prevented this. It is not always possible to anticipate when people are going to drink too much, but when they have, the best thing is to cut off contact with them as quickly and as diplomatically as possible, even where a business situation is involved. They remember very little the next day, anyhow.

                    ✓      ✓      ✓

I am a young man who is frequently invited to be an extra man at dinner parties, theater parties, etc., in our city. As I work long hours in a bank, I never have time to make the party calls my mother taught me were essential. I know many men accept these invitations without ever attempting to return them or even bothering to thank their hostesses, except at the time of the entertainment. Could you set me right? J.M.W., Pasadena, California

The eligible young man is certainly at a premium today in many cities. He is likely to become spoiled by social attention of the kind you mention being showered upon him. In more leisured times he would, as you know, have paid a party call the next day, or as soon as possible, upon his hostess. But today she is probably not in to receive such a party call, should he attempt one. Therefore, the courteous young man does call her on the phone within a reasonable time, or drop her a note, or—nicest of all—send her flowers with his personal card, on which he has written a few sincere words of appreciation. While hostesses need attractive bachelors to fill in on such occasions, they come eventually to resent even the most attractive ones who continuously take and rarely reciprocate in any way.

*        *        *

My sister claims it is impolite to thank anyone for a meal. For instance, if a friend takes you to lunch, you must not thank her for the luncheon, or if you are invited to a home to dine, you must not thank the hostess for the nice dinner. What is your opinion? G.J.S., Los Angeles, California

Today, people do thank their hosts and hostesses for the "nice luncheon" or for the "lovely dinner." They even comment on the food itself if it has been unusual. Most hostesses are flattered by such attention from their guests. But the idea behind your sister's remark goes back to the days when it was considered somewhat indelicate for a lady, in particular, to concern herself about eating. She had to pretend an elaborate disinterest in food. Days might have been spent on the preparation of a great dinner, but guests were considered ill-bred if they mentioned it specifically in thanking their host for entertainment. What still should be avoided is what might be called the "overly hungry" attitude toward such entertainment. A guest should never give the impression that he comes only to eat, that the food is a prime consideration in the acceptance of the entertainment.

*        *        *

Recently I was a house guest, and my host and hostess had made a reservation at a restaurant for dinner. As I was dressing, friends of theirs arrived. My host and hostess explained that we were getting ready to go out, but the friends made no move to go. How should this situation have been handled? My hostess felt that she should stay and entertain her friends as long as they remained. Mrs. G.M.B., Los Angeles, California

Your hostess should have said to her friends, "I'm so sorry. We didn't know that you were coming. We have made a reservation for dinner and are due there in half an hour. In the meantime, it will be very nice talking to you." Friends who don't realize that their host and hostess owe them no obligation when they drop in casually like this, when prior arrangements have been made, are thick-skinned indeed. Certainly your friends had no obligation, either to stay home and entertain the "drop-ins" or to invite them to join you at the restaurant at their expense. Their obligation was to you as their properly invited guest.

*     *     *

When I was a girl the only proper guest towel was a linen one. However, when I go to my friends' houses I find in the bathroom for guests towels of paper and fingertip towels of turkish toweling, as well as the more familiar small linen towels. Do you approve of this? F.J.L., Chicago, Illinois

Very much so. It is very nice to have a full complement of small guest towels in the bathroom in linen, but it is wise to have a pile of the pretty, individual paper towels that are soft and pliable as well as decorative. Men in particular like to use the little turkish fingertip towels because of their easy absorbency. A roll of paper toweling is fine for children.

## PARTIES, SPECIAL OCCASIONS, AND CELEBRATIONS

Please advise me concerning entertaining at Christmas. This being our first year settled in our home, my husband and I wish to begin to have open house at Christmas for our friends every year. What day would be best? I hope to have approximately fifty guests. Mrs. R.W., Kansas City, Missouri

Many people like to entertain on Christmas Eve, New Year's Eve, or New Year's Day at an open house. It is nice for a young couple such as you are to pick a day the first year of your marriage and plan to make it a regular occasion. The custom of social calling has been greatly neglected the last generation, but many people throughout the country consider New Year's Day one on which a call should be made on as many close friends and acquaintances as possible. So whether or not you have an open house at some other time during the holidays, it is probable that on New Year's Day, if you are at home, you will receive some calls.

✦ ✦ ✦

**We have moved into a new neighborhood and are going to have a housewarming. Should we invite neighbors we haven't met yet? Mrs. G.T., Trenton, New Jersey**

No, invite just your friends. Generally speaking, you should wait for your neighbors to call upon you before extending them any invitations.

✦ ✦ ✦

**May you issue invitations for dinner and parties by phone or in person? If so, how do you go about it? E.S., Brookfield, Connecticut**

Yes. You say, "Will you come to dinner on Tuesday, the eighth, at seven. It will be quite informal."

✦ ✦ ✦

**Soon my husband and I will be moving from a three-room apartment to a new six-room house. We would like very much to give a housewarming sometime after we are all settled. Just how long after is it permissible to give such a thing? What refreshments are served, and, most important, is it possible to put in our invitations, "No gifts, please?" I have heard there are gifts for the new home generally brought to housewarmings, and I don't want anyone to feel obligated to bring us a gift. Also, as we are young and just starting out, we won't be able to have rugs in all of the rooms right away. Should we hold up our housewarming because of this? Mrs. F.R.M., Bound Brook, New Jersey**

Have your housewarming, rugs or not, and at any time that is convenient for you. The housewarming may include a buffet supper or may be a tea or cocktail party—in fact, any kind of entertainment you wish. Say nothing about gifts. Some people will bring them to the house, and others may not know of this custom. Where some bring gifts and others do not, it is courteous of the hostess to put aside the gifts some do bring, for later opening. Gifts should be acknowledged by a brief note as soon as possible.

ᕗ   ᕗ   ᕗ

My three sisters-in-law and I would like to show our affection for our father-in-law by entertaining for him on his eighty-fifth birthday. "Open house" here in our Nebraska town is an informal afternoon tea, with anyone who would like to come invited. As our father-in-law is an early settler, we hope nearly everyone in the community will do him honor. Occasionally we see announcements for such things in the newspapers here, but someone has raised the question, "Is it proper?" Sometimes the announcements say, "Please do not bring gifts." Mrs. J.B.K., Lexington, Nebraska

Yes, it is proper to give an announcement to the society editor of your local paper concerning your "open house," and while I think you should let the news get around that you do not expect gifts, I would rather not see it in the announcement in this way. Most people know that gifts are not expected on such occasions except perhaps from those very near and dear.

ᕗ   ᕗ   ᕗ

My daughter's family lost all of their belongings in a fire a year ago. Now they are moving into a new house by Christmas. May they have a housewarming, or should some member of the family give it for them? R.U., Chattanooga, Tennessee

They give it themselves in most communities.

ᕗ   ᕗ   ᕗ

My fiancé is hoping to be granted his naturalization shortly. If and when he becomes a citizen, I plan to invite a few friends to my house to celebrate the occasion. Will you please let me know the procedure for the invitations and the party? Would it be proper for his friends and myself to present him with a gift and if so, what would be appropriate? Miss L.P.E., Sarasota, Florida

It is nice to want to give a party for a newly naturalized citizen. You just do this as you would make arrangements for any other informal party, inviting his close friends and yours. At the party you might have some male friend propose a toast to the new American. I wouldn't specify the reason for the party, necessarily. You would invite people by phone, by note, or, if it's a cocktail party, you could use little cocktail cards. You could give your friend a gift—something that would make his life smoother here might be nice—our flag, a good dictionary or an American etiquette book, for example.

## GIFTS

When you are a week-end guest, are you supposed to take a gift to the hostess, to the family as a whole, to the children, if any? D.S., Salt Lake City, Utah

If you are a frequent guest in the household, you take gifts from time to time, not necessarily on every visit. When there are young children they are often disappointed not to receive something from a guest—and the gift may be very modest indeed to please a child—colored pencils (especially with his name on them), a rubber ball, a little toy. A gift to the whole family may of course include the children and is often something like candy. A gift for the hostess may well be something for the house or a book that appeals to her reading tastes. A woman may give wearing apparel to the hostess but a man guest should not (unless he's a relative) give anything so intimate as stockings or lingerie. A woman guest who does not know her hostess well also avoids gifts that are intimate.

✓   ✓   ✓

My husband and I and our two small children are planning on visiting friends in another part of the country whom we have not seen for three years. There are also several other families with whom we will be staying, and we would like to compensate them for their hospitality. They are all hard-working people and we wonder would it be bad to send a gift of appreciation after we come home, buy them something for their home the second or third day of our visit, or should we simply leave a gift of money in an inconspicuous spot? We have never been able to entertain them overnight. Mrs. Z.H., Phoenix, Arizona

You may take them each some gift from your own home town which might be unusual to them, or, as you suggest, get them some gift you see that they might enjoy the second or third day of your visit, or you may send them something after you reach home again. By no means leave them a gift of money. This is only appropriate when there are domestics to be compensated for extra work guests cause on overnight, or longer, visits.

✓    ✓    ✓

I have been dating a girl for ten months. I plan to give her a Christmas present, but should I include her father and mother too? I have been entertained in their home many times, and they are very friendly toward me. T.R.S., Pasadena, California

It would be nice to give the girl's mother an impersonal gift or to give some small gift to the household which the father and mother will both enjoy. If Christmas giving is a strain financially, you could do this at any time during the year. You would, of course, very probably send a Christmas card to the girl's parents.

✓    ✓    ✓

I am a man invited to spend Christmas Day with a family in the country. There are three small children, a husband and wife. I am an old friend of the wife's but know the husband slightly. What gifts am I expected to take? M.R.K., Erie, Pennsylvania

If the children are so young that they dislike sharing presents, you might take a small gift to each, not necessarily expensive. You could then take an impersonal gift of some kind to your hostess, the pleasure of which her husband would share. Perhaps salted nuts, a box of candied fruits, a bottle of wine, or any one of a number of things for the house. In this category come bar accessories, basic books, such as new cookbooks, books that fit in with the family's hobbies if you know them, flowers, house plants, or games.

## MEAL SERVICE

**The subject of demitasse has always confused me. If guests prefer coffee with their meal is it proper to serve demitasse afterward? Is it served at the table after the completion of the dinner or after the guests have been seated in the living room? In the latter case is it correct to serve a liqueur with the demitasse? K.W.T., New Orleans, Louisiana**

If all the guests have had coffee at dinner, it is certainly not necessary to serve demitasse after dinner, although it would be nice if everybody is particularly enthusiastic about coffee. You may serve a liqueur, of course, after dinner even when demitasse is not offered. Where you have served demitasse, guests may be offered liqueurs after demitasse has been served to everyone present. As some people like to add liqueur brandy to their demitasse, the liqueur service should not be delayed too long after the coffee has been passed. It is correct today, by the way, to offer cream with demitasse, as many people like it that way. It is considerate to have a decaffeinated coffee available should anyone prefer it.

*✓      ✓      ✓*

**We frequently entertain buffet style for supper or dinner. I am expecting a new baby and already have two others. Most of my guests are eager to help me, but some never offer to. In this instance, could I go ahead and start cleaning up alone? I wouldn't want them to think I would rather wash dishes than be with them. Mrs. G.A.G., Fort Worth, Texas**

Don't worry about them. Think about yourself. It is good for you to have guests, but not if they make too much work when you have no help. If you know yours are the non-helping kind of guests, serve them as informally as possible—use paper cups and plates—

and don't apologize. And enlist your husband's aid in the serving and cleaning up after the meal.

✓  ✓  ✓

A friend tells me it is bad manners to serve vegetables in individual vegetable dishes at a home table the way they do in restaurants. Is that right? Mrs. B.B.G., Charlotte, North Carolina

Vegetables aren't served this way in first-class restaurants. Instead, the waiter serves them onto the diner's plate from a serving dish. At a family dinner, something like stewed tomatoes could be served in separate vegetable dishes, but in more formal service the vegetable is always taken onto the dinner or luncheon plate. Of course you can always serve a vegetable as a separate course, European style. Asparagus hollandaise is nice this way and so is creamed spinach with croutons. They are served before the meat.

✓  ✓  ✓

Recently a friend gave me a lace tablecloth which is very beautiful. This particular cloth is machine-made as distinguished from a handmade type. I would like your advice on the proper times to use it. Would it be appropriate for all or some of these four occasions:

1. Everyday dinner, just for the family.
2. Everyday luncheon.
3. Dinner with guests invited.
4. A buffet table setting.

Mrs. S.F.K., Houston, Texas

A lace cloth is always much more formal than a plain one of any kind. Therefore, it is suitable for dinner with guests and for a buffet table setting and should be accompanied by fine silver, china, and crystal. It should always be laid on a bare table (see page 60). It does not lend itself well to informal table accessories such as earthenware, wood, and stainless steel.

✓  ✓  ✓

Do salad bowls and iced-tea glasses require service plates beneath them? T.W., Long Beach, California

A salad bowl does not require a service plate beneath it, nor does an iced-tea glass, although in the latter case, if you wish, you may have one, and then the spoon may be placed upon it rather than left in the glass while one is drinking, necessary when there is no service plate beneath it. In the latter case, one uses the index finger to hold the spoon against the side of the glass as the tea is drunk.

❦        ❦        ❦

**I have parfait glasses and sometimes like to serve a parfait for dessert. I have no parfait spoons. Would it be all right to use iced-tea spoons instead, and do you think a parfait makes a nice company dessert?** Mrs. G.W., Lyons, New York

Yes to both questions.

❦        ❦        ❦

**May candles ever be lighted on a dining table in the daytime?** A.V.L., Maplewood, New York

No, except late in the day and if the curtains are drawn. Candles placed on the table to be lighted at a later hour, as the tea or reception wears on, should have their wicks charred.

❦        ❦        ❦

**When just our family eats together we seldom put water on the table except at Sunday dinner when we are a little more formal. The children have milk and my husband and I have coffee and, as we don't drink the water even if we do put it on, I like to save myself trouble. In the summertime, however, when we serve iced tea or iced coffee when guests are present, should I put on the water glasses, too—and what is the appropriate glass?** G.M.B., Baltimore, Maryland

Technically, even when iced coffee or iced tea is served, a water glass is placed at the point of the knife. At lunch and dinner the proper glass is a stem goblet, not a tumbler, which is the right one to use at breakfast. However, as most households don't make any attempt anymore at formal service, water glasses may be omitted at a family meal at which guests are present if iced tea or iced coffee is served. If, however, you are setting your table with wine glasses, be sure to include the water goblet, too, as some guests may not take the wine and will certainly want something to drink. Water, by the way, is poured before the guests are seated. The glasses are replenished as needed throughout the meal from a pitcher of ice water on the serving table or sideboard—or even on the table itself if there is plenty of room. When the water pitcher is on the table, the guests serve themselves additional water as desired. When there are no servants and the water pitcher is on the sideboard, the hostess watches to see when guests may need more water and passes them the pitcher so that they may serve themselves.

✓　　✓　　✓

**I'm writing you for information regarding the serving of frozen foods which are packaged in foil tins. I am referring particularly to individual meat pies which are purchased and baked in foil containers. Should they be removed from the containers or served in them? Is it proper to place the baked pie, still in its foil, on the dinner plate to be eaten from the container? Would it be better to place the pie in the foil on a bread and butter plate beside the dinner plate with a serving spoon for one to serve himself? Mrs. F.E.A., Brattleboro, Vermont**

No, you do not remove the baked pies from the foil containers when you serve individual pies. Because the pies are served hot, it is easier to place them individually on dinner plates and then place the dinner plates in front of the diners. The vegetables are then passed separately.

In the case of individual dessert pies, again, I would heat them in the oven, place them on dessert plates, and serve them that way instead of asking the diners to try to manipulate them with serving spoons and forks, as this might prove disastrous.

✓　　✓　　✓

**We are going to entertain the parents of my daughter's fiancé at dinner. How should I seat the six of us at table? Mrs. L.R., Norwalk, Connecticut**

You seat the father of your daughter's fiancé at your right and your future son-in-law at your left. To your husband's right sits the mother of your fiancé and to his left sits your daughter.

✓　　✓　　✓

I know it is supposed to be proper for one to seat the next most honored male guest to the hostess's left. But I have a very small boy, age three, who, with our older daughter, has dinner with us. I like to have the little boy next to me so that I can supervise his eating and keep him from being a nuisance. Is this all right? And if a man and his wife are our guests, how should I seat everybody at table? Mrs. J.K., Syracuse, New York

As a mother myself, I understand your dilemma. I think you are wise to keep your smaller child next to you, on your left. You would then seat your male guest to your right and his wife to the host's right, with your daughter to her father's left. However, if your woman guest is rather unfamiliar with the ways of children and seems a little nervous at sitting next to the baby, you might ask her if she prefers to sit at your husband's left and have the two children sit together at the same side of the table. I know some of my readers might suggest that the children eat by themselves at an earlier hour. This is the better solution, of course, but doesn't always work out in a household where there is no servant, especially if the children are used to eating with their parents. I recommend that children eat with both parents and guests as soon as they are able to do so without unduly upsetting the guests, for this is the best social training for them. However, one must pick one's guests, under the circumstances, very carefully.

_✓ ✓ ✓_

When you have no maid, where is the best place to put the dessert silver? I find that if I put a dessert spoon with the soup spoon and the dinner knife sometimes people pick it up when they mean to pick up the soup spoon. Then when the dessert course comes, I have to replace the dessert spoon, which sometimes embarrasses the guest. Mrs. L.O., Providence, Rhode Island

The best way I think to place dessert silver informally when there is no maid—and sometimes when there is one—is to place it above the dinner plate. If a spoon and fork are both needed (when the dessert is at all liquid) they are placed in the manner shown in the illustration. The dessert silver, of course, may also be brought in on the filled dessert dishes, spoon (if needed) on the right,

fork on the left. Or if the hostess is serving the dessert from her
place she may bring in the dessert silver and place it in a pattern
at her right, adding it to the dishes as she fills them.

INFORMAL PLACEMENT OF DESSERT SILVER, informal lunch and dinner:
This is a convenient way to place dessert silver above the place plate.
Without first course (or with first course served after guests are seated):
Dinner napkin is on dinner plate (or on service plate if one is used)
when guests sit down, as at a formal dinner. Note optional placement
of dessert silver, easy when service is limited or when serving is done
by the hostess.

On a properly set table for dinner, where does the napkin go (1)
When there is already a course in place when the guests sit down?
(2) When there is a service plate but no first course in place?
Mrs. J.J.M., Tulsa, Oklahoma

When there is a course in place as the guests sit down, the napkin
is at the left of the place setting. When there is no first course on
the service plate, the dinner napkin is laid on the plate itself or
folded in any of the ways that permit it to stand upright. See
illustration at top of following page.

**I would like to be able to serve tea more often. But it always seems so complicated. Could you tell me just how to go about it so I'll have more confidence?** R.C., Jamaica, New York

I think the best way is to give you this information in the following illustration. The great secret in successful tea serving, of course, is to let the water boil actively three or four minutes. It is then poured immediately over the tea leaves—one teaspoon of tea for each cup and one for the pot. And the pot should be scalded first. Some dry it out before adding the tea. For the tea tray setting see the illustration. A spirit lamp keeps the tea hot but is not essential if a tea pot which retains the heat well is selected.

**When there is a dinner at which there are both men and women guests and the hostess has no one to help her serve, what does she do when everybody offers to help her at once when the time has come to remove a course?** Mrs. J.V.L., Montgomery, Alabama

She can designate one or more friends to help her, choosing those who seem more familiar with the procedure. An eager but dish-happy bachelor can break a lot of your best china. The hostess is firm about not permitting the entire table to rise and march toward the kitchen, as this breaks up all semblance of conversation. I feel strongly that a hostess without help should make her parties as simple as possible, and in this instance an efficient hostess can clear the table herself with the help of a serving table, often, actually, without even leaving the table if she has managed it well. She lets her guests pass their soiled dishes to her and she places these on the lower shelf of the table, scraping where necessary very unobtrusively. She then takes the next course off the top of the serving table, if it has been possible to arrange it there. At any rate she cuts down her trips to the kitchen to an absolute minimum. If she prefers to clear alone she may always say so, and guests should follow her request.

✓ ✓ ✓

**At what point are the candles lighted on a table—before the guests sit down or after they are seated? When are they extinguished?** L.D., Portland, Oregon

They are lighted by the hostess or by a servant just before the guests enter the dining room. They are extinguished after the guests have left the table and it is about to be cleared.

✓ ✓ ✓

**I am never quite sure how to use place cards—and when. How are names properly written upon them?** L.E., Troy, New York

Place cards are a convenience to the hostess who is seating more than eight guests. They may be used at any time—at a festive breakfast, at luncheon, at seated buffet suppers, and, of course, at large formal dinners. For family affairs, birthday or holiday parties, the familiar decorated cards are quite permissible, with first names, if desired, written in black ink, "Julie" or "Tom," but formal place cards follow a prescribed pattern. For example, titles at diplomatic dinners are abbreviated, "H.E. [for His Excellency] the Norwegian Ambassador," and other place card names are written simply "Mrs. Roberts," "Miss Sweeney," etc. Place cards, if flat, are propped against a standing dinner napkin or laid on a folded one. Or they may be placed above the place plate. If the double cards are used they are set above the place setting.

✶ ✶ ✶

**When you use a lace tablecloth do you lay it directly over the table or on a table pad? Is a lace tablecloth ever used with a colored lining? Mrs. M.McN., Ozone Park, New York**

You use a lace tablecloth directly over the bare table. As the lace design is decoration enough, it is better taste not to put it over a colored lining.

✶ ✶ ✶

**Often when I entertain, my table or buffet is quite crowded with platters of food and I don't have room for a bread dish. Since I do want to serve rolls with dinner, would it be possible for me to have rolls and butter already on the butter plates before the guests are seated? Mrs. B.R., Youngstown, Ohio.**

Yes. This is a solution often used even in formal service.

# ENGAGEMENTS
# AND WEDDINGS

## *Dear Miss Vanderbilt:*

### ENGAGEMENTS

I understand that when an engagement is announced, the boy's parents call as soon as possible upon the parents of the girl. But my case is very difficult. My daughter, who is announcing her engagement, lives with me, and I am divorced from her father, who lives in the same town. We are fairly friendly. Would it be expected of us to receive this call together at my home? Should they ignore my daughter's father or call on him separately? D.W.W., Columbus, Georgia

Receive their call without your former husband. They may call on your daughter's father separately if he is still very much part of all of your lives. If they do call, they call jointly, or the boy's father may call alone on your former husband and perhaps, during the call, arrange for him to come and meet the new family. Even if your relations with your former husband are friendly, you should not make the traditional return visit a joint one.

*✓    ✓    ✓*

How does a father announce the engagement of his daughter to a gathering of relatives and friends at home? Is a toast in order? C.B.C., St. Petersburg, Florida

Yes. After all have assembled and the party is well under way, the father, first catching everyone's attention, proposes a toast. Sometimes if champagne has not been served up to this point it is brought out and ceremoniously poured. When everyone has been served, the father raises his glass and says something like this: "To my daughter Margaret and my future son-in-law John. Let us drink to their happiness."

✔   ✔   ✔

My daughter, who is in her first year of college, has just become engaged to a boy in the service. He has three years more to go, the first half to be spent overseas. They plan to marry in three or four years. We like the boy very much but, in view of the length of time involved, I feel that no announcement of the engagement should be made now. Am I right? A.C.R., Duluth, Minnesota

A great deal can happen in three or four years, especially with young people separated. What they both think they want now may not be at all what they want at the end of that time. Therefore, do not announce the engagement, and try to persuade them to leave each other free until it is practical to speak of a wedding date.

✔   ✔   ✔

My fiancé and I work together in this city, but we are going to my home, several states distant, to be married. Is it all right for us to travel together in the train without a chaperone? It is an overnight trip. R.W., Cleveland, Ohio

Yes, but preferably you occupy quarters in separate cars, and of course you observe all proprieties. The other people in the train are now considered proper chaperones for you.

✔   ✔   ✔

Before my fiancé went to Alaska, we decided to wait until he got back to marry, but, as he has been gone two years, it seems a long time. Would it be good taste if I should go to him? He is sending me the money for the trip. L.V.B., West Orange, New Jersey

It is quite proper for you to go to him. However, just in case the marriage should not take place after you arrive, you should, for his protection and your own, pay your own passage, borrowing the money for the purpose if necessary. After the marriage, he can then reimburse you and you can then repay the loan if it was necessary to make one.

✓       ✓       ✓

**My daughter is going to marry a man who cannot afford to give her an engagement ring. Should she announce the engagement when she has no ring, and should her friends give showers for her?** A.L.H., Pensacola, Florida

Yes to both questions. Sometimes engagement rings are not given and other gifts are given by the boy instead. Or the girl may choose a wedding ring that is a combination engagement and wedding ring—perhaps it will have some stones in it, not necessarily diamonds, or it may be decorated in some other way. Above all, she should not apologize for not having an engagement ring nor imply that the boy cannot afford one.

✓       ✓       ✓

**Our daughter has just become engaged, and we would like to announce the event through the newspapers. Are there any special rules to be followed? Do you suggest we send pictures?** Mrs. C.McK., Provincetown, Massachusetts

Be sure your story follows the basic rule of journalism so that when completed it answers the questions, "who, what, when, where, and how?" Here is an engagement announcement that answers the newsman's questions:

### CYNTHIA ANN TALBOTT
### TO WED ASA G. SANTOS

Mr. and Mrs. Loring Talbott, of 10 Low Place, announce the engagement of their daughter, Cynthia Ann, to Mr. Asa Griggs Santos, son of Dr. and Mrs. José Santos of Mexico City, Mexico.

Miss Talbott is a graduate of Miss Hewitt's Classes and of Vassar College. Mr. Santos is a senior in the Yale School of Medicine and a member of Phi Beta Kappa. He will intern at Lying-in Hospital, Boston. The wedding will take place in June.

If you wish, send a picture of the engaged girl with the announcement. It should have a caption attached with the typed information, "Miss Cynthia Ann Talbott whose engagement to Mr. Asa G. Santos has been announced," on a piece of 8"×10" typewriter paper. Enclose picture, with a protective cardboard and the release, in a mailing envelope and send "special" to papers or have delivered by hand to either city or society desk as the news seems to warrant.

✓        ✓        ✓

I am planning to be married soon. It will be a second marriage for me—his first. We are planning a small, quiet ceremony with only close members of the family and one or two good friends. However, there is little or no information available about announcing the wedding. Is any sort of engagement notice proper in the newspaper? I believe, after the wedding, announcements should be sent to people directly concerned. Can you help us? Mrs. D.L.E., Waukegan, Illinois

Brides who have been previously divorced usually do not announce their engagements, except informally to close friends and relatives. The exception might be in the unusual newsworthiness of one or the other of the parties or in the case of a very young divorcée, divorced without scandal, remarrying. Then the new engagement is sometimes announced by the parents of the bride. Announcements are sent after the ceremony.

✓        ✓        ✓

We are having a party—not at home—to be held in honor of an engagement. We have been advised that we should have a receiving line, as many of the guests have not met either set of parents personally. If we should have a receiving line, what is the proper order? L.K.M., Hays, Kansas

An engagement party, when given at all, is essentially an informal occasion. It does not call for a receiving line. Although it is to be held away from home, presumably in a public place, the matter can be handled very simply. The party will probably be given by the parents of the engaged girl, and the announcement of the engagement will be made by the father during the evening in a toast to the young couple. If all of the guests know the occasion for the party, the young couple may choose to receive together, just inside the door—the girl first, then her fiancé. They will greet their guests informally, just as they will in their future home. As the opportunity arises, they introduce their guests to the two sets of parents, or, if many people arrive at one time, guests may always introduce themselves to each other and to the parents.

*        *        *

**When does my fiancé give me my engagement ring—while we are alone, or in front of our guests at the engagement party?** M.B.R., Pittsburgh, Pennsylvania

He should give you your ring in private.

*        *        *

**What sort of gift should I give my fiancé? I have a better-paying job than he has and wish I could add to the sum he can spend for my ring so I can have one that's a little better. Do you think it would be right to suggest such a thing?** L.S.E., Pueblo, Colorado

Do not minimize your fiancé's gift of the ring he can afford by giving him anything too costly as an engagement gift. A pair of cuff links, your portrait in a nice, masculine frame, or some other well-chosen gift that he'll keep for life is suitable. As for suggesting you pay for part of the ring, don't. If you feel two rings would be a real problem financially, suggest the kind of jeweled wedding band that will double for engagement ring and wedding ring. Tell your friends that this is your preference, but do not wear the ring until your wedding day.

*        *        *

**I am planning on becoming engaged soon. When I was sixteen, I inherited a diamond ring. Would it be proper for my fiancé to have the diamond reset for me to wear as an engagement ring?** J.R., Buffalo, New York

Yes. It would be quite all right for you to wear your family's heirloom. Your fiancé, however, should pay for the resetting.

*        *        *

What is the current attitude on the type of stone which is suitable for an engagement ring? Must it be a diamond, or can a man give a different type of stone and still not be accused of ignorance? M.L., Jr., Reading, Pennsylvania

A diamond is the traditional engagement stone, but any other stone is suitable. A girl with a large hand and long fingers might be much happier with a square-cut tourmaline than with a miniscule diamond. And many modern girls like the idea of a gem-studded wedding band which combines engagement and wedding ring in one. Some girls even forego an engagement ring in favor of some other keepsake, such as a bracelet or a pin. The important thing in the matter is that the ring, if given, should not be so costly that it is all out of proportion to the man's income. An heirloom ring can be very valuable, and any girl should be proud to be given one. But no girl should place a burden on her fiancé in the purchase of a ring which he cannot really afford.

⚹     ⚹     ⚹

I have just become engaged, and my mother says I should be engaged for a year before I get married. Do you think this is necessary? Miss M.T., Phoenix, Arizona

Today the usual engagement runs approximately three months but of course may be either a shorter or longer period of time. Over-long engagements are now unusual.

⚹     ⚹     ⚹

I have just broken my engagement. What do I do about gifts and money that I have received from friends and relatives? Should I return them? How should I explain about my broken engagement? Miss V.G., Santa Barbara, California

Yes, you should return the gifts and money. It isn't necessary to make any explanation of your broken engagement except that you have broken it by mutual consent.

⚹     ⚹     ⚹

My son recently gave a diamond to a girl who lives in another state. I have met her parents but once. Will you please answer the following questions? Mrs. R.M., Hollywood, California

1. Do I write to the parents, the girl, or neither? A: You write to the parents and to the girl separately.

2. The girl has attended college for two years in the city where my son has lived his entire life. Is it proper for me to plan an affair for all his friends and relations so they may meet his new bride when they are married? A: If you mean that she is to be married in her home state and will return to yours, yes. It is proper and cordial of you to sponsor some occasion at which she will meet all of the immediate friends of the family and relatives. Unless she is coming directly from her wedding she should not wear her wedding veil. She may wear her wedding dress.

3. Should this affair be at the home of the groom or in a clubhouse or church? A: At the home of the groom or in a clubhouse or anywhere else you would be likely to entertain.

4. Are presents expected or displayed? A: No, the bride will have received her gifts at her own home.

5. Should there be a receiving line? If so, who should be in it? A: It depends on the formality of the occasion. If you have an actual reception, you as hostess should be first in line, followed by the bride, her mother, her father, and if the occasion is very formal, the groom's father. The groom, presumably knowing everyone present, would circulate as host, and, except under formal circumstances, so would his father.

6. What kind of invitations or announcements are sent? A: No announcements are sent by you, but you may invite people by phone, personal note, or by wire.

✓   ✓   ✓

My daughter's engagement was just announced, and we are planning to send the information to our local newspaper. Her fiancé is an excellent amateur photographer and has taken some rather lovely formal photographs of her. Would one of these be suitable to send to the papers or must these pictures be taken professionally? Mrs. L.T., Coral Gables, Florida

Any picture taken for use as an engagement or bridal picture should be a professionally taken formal pose. The candid pictures often taken at wedding receptions should also be taken by professionals so that friends may enjoy themselves and not worry about "working" during a wedding. This way, too, the bride can be sure she will have her wedding recorded in good pictures.

## SHOWERS

**Should the bride-to-be, after opening all the gifts at a bridal shower, go on to the envelope gifts (money) and read the amount or not? Many of us think she should, because when a gift is opened all the people see it and almost everyone can guess, or already knows, what it costs. Therefore, I think the bride should say, "Three dollars, five dollars, or ten dollars from so-and-so," instead of "Money from so-and-so." Lots of people get offended that way if they don't tell the amount. What do you think? Miss M.S.T., Reading, Pennsylvania**

Whether or not a money gift to the bride-to-be is in the form of a check or in cash, the rule remains the same: The donor is disclosed conversationally; i.e. "Father gave us a check." But later in any display of wedding gifts it is proper only to say, perhaps on a card propped up, "Check, $100.00," without the name of the donor. This is done to save the feelings of those who cannot in any way meet the amount named in their own giving. Besides, any very obvious discussion of money under social circumstances is considered bad taste. No bride would ever say, for example, "This is a silver tray Aunt Mary gave us. I know it cost $500 at Tiffany's."

✓     ✓     ✓

**I have been asked to be maid of honor for a friend and would like to give her a shower. However, a large party was given for her by her family to announce the engagement. Many of her friends took beautiful gifts to her at that time—some of them quite expensive. She is going to have a large wedding with a reception, and the majority of these same people will send presents.**

I feel it would be an imposition to ask them all to contribute a third gift, and I myself being in modest financial circumstances would like to avoid the expense I would have to go to in giving her a shower, the cost of a special dress, etc. May I have your opinion? Miss L.T.S., Dallas, Texas

You are not obligated to give her a shower, especially as it would be a strain on you and perhaps upon her already generous friends.

✓    ✓    ✓

I work in an office where, when a girl gets married, we collect money and give her a gift which is sometimes presented to her at a shower. Now, if she invites me to the wedding with an individual invitation, does this mean another gift just from me? J.L.H., Providence, Rhode Island

No, even though you go to the wedding you need not send an additional wedding gift if you have contributed to the one given by the office force.

✓    ✓    ✓

A friend of mine has been reared by her paternal grandmother who wants to give a bridal shower for her. But the girl's sister, who will be maid of honor, also wants to give the shower. The grandmother is willing to share expenses. Who should give it? Mrs. R.G., Pittsburgh, Pennsylvania

Neither. No member of the family should give a shower for the bride. A bridal shower should be given by a friend rather than a relative because, if a relative gives it, it looks as if the family actually is asking for gifts for the bride. However, there is no reason why both sister and grandmother could not quietly share in any of the shower expenses, either by supplying some of the food or in defraying some of the cost.

✓    ✓    ✓

My girl friend and I received an invitation from two girls we know to a shower they are giving in a restaurant. We were shocked when we read the invitation. At the end it went something like this: "Buffet supper—$1.50 fee." I have never seen anything like this. Is it proper? K.W., Paterson, New Jersey

No, it isn't. A shower is properly given in the home of a friend of the bride-to-be. It should not be commercialized in such a manner as this.

✓   ✓   ✓

Both my little girl, eleven and a half years old, and myself have been invited to the shower of a young cousin by marriage. I have also been invited to the wedding and have ordered a gift to be sent. I feel that neither my daughter nor I should have been invited to this shower as there is such a difference in our ages in relation to that of the engaged girl. Should I send a gift to the shower if we don't go? D.L.S., Chicago, Illinois

I agree that neither of you should have been invited to the shower because of the difference in your ages from that of the bride and her friends. You are not obliged to send a gift, although you should let them know if you are not going. The wedding gift you are sending is certainly sufficient.

## ARRANGING THE WEDDING

Our local church is fairly large, but I am having a simple wedding with few guests. Must the church be completely decorated with flowers? Should I have the aisle carpeted? Do I need a canopy out to the street? A.C.M., Lancaster, Pennsylvania

You may limit the flowers, if you wish, to suitable ones for the altar. Even very formal weddings frequently do not use the canopy anymore. It is not necessary to have the church aisle carpeted, but, if you decide to do so, this is taken care of by the florist who decorates the church.

✓   ✓   ✓

Is it possible to have a widow or a divorcée as a matron of honor? Is it all right if some of the bridesmaids are married? And if they are married, must one have their husbands as ushers? L.S.W., Wichita, Kansas

The matron of honor may be a widow, but it is preferable that she not be a divorcée or very much older than the bride. Bridesmaids may be married, but it is unusual, though not really incorrect, for them to serve with their husbands. Incidentally, married men who serve as ushers or attendants must have their wives invited to the ceremony and of course to the reception.

✓   ✓   ✓

**Someone told me that it is not good taste to get married on Sunday. If it isn't, why isn't it? A.R.R., Somerville, New Jersey**

Ministers tell me that it is less customary for people to be married on their own Sabbath because their clergymen are fully occupied on that day and the church is being used for religious services. Aside from this, there is nothing really against being married on the Sabbath. Jews often marry on Sunday, which is not their own Sabbath. Sunday Christian marriages are almost the rule in some parts of the South.

✓   ✓   ✓

**I am planning to be married in our own small church where the minister has known me since babyhood. I understand that under ordinary circumstances my fiancé and I should visit the minister to discuss the details of the ceremony and any church regulations that must be fulfilled. Also so the minister can see if he approves of my husband-to-be. But as they have met many times socially, couldn't my mother make the church arrangements, as I work every day? G.A.T., Phoenix, Arizona**

Yes, under these circumstances your mother could make the arrangements. Try to have a conference with the minister, however, sometime before the marriage, taking your fiancé with you, so that the minister may be fully satisfied that you are both taking the right step.

✓   ✓   ✓

**My husband and I are invited to an out-of-town wedding, but he will be unable to go. Would it be correct for my son, a college freshman in school near the city where the wedding will take place, to meet me and go as my escort? Mrs. W.J.M., Berwyn, Illinois**

Yes. You would reply to the invitation this way:

*Mrs. Ronald Gordon Smith*
*and Mr. Ronald Gordon Smith, Jr.*
*accept with pleasure*
*the kind invitation of*
*Mr. and Mrs. Jones*
*for Saturday, the third of November*
*at eight o'clock*
*Mr. Ronald Gordon Smith*
*will not be able to attend.*

✓     ✓     ✓

**Who should I choose as my best man? I live with my married sister and her husband. My future wife, my sister and her husband and I have gone out socially many times. Considering my fiancée has only one brother and I have none, I wonder if he should be my choice, although I don't know him well. Who would be a logical choice? R.P., Waco, Texas**

Your sister's husband, unless you have a very close friend whom you would prefer to have and providing there is not too great a difference in age. Very occasionally, especially if he has no brother, the groom asks his father to be his best man. If the father is very young-looking this does not seem too incongruous, but it is best to keep the wedding party at the same age level as that of the bride and groom.

✓     ✓     ✓

**A few days ago I received an invitation to a wedding containing a stamped, addressed response card. Quite honestly I was insulted that these people didn't think I would answer their invitation on my own. Were they correct? F.M.P., Juneau, Alaska**

This practice, although practical, is not socially acceptable. The only instance when it should be used is with the issuing of formal *business* invitations.

✓     ✓     ✓

**I am going to be a bridesmaid and have never been one before. Am I expected to buy my own dress? And how do I get to the church? G.C.F., Garden City, New York**

Today's bridesmaid nearly always buys her own clothes, but she wears what the bride selects, of course, so that all the bridesmaids may be dressed alike. Bridesmaids assemble at the home of the bride a full hour before the ceremony. They may arrive dressed, or dress after they reach the bride's home. They receive their bouquets, and transportation is provided for them from the bride's home to the church.

✝   ✝   ✝

**I am going to have my little sister, aged fourteen, as a junior bridesmaid. Must I have a maid or matron of honor as well, and where does she stand in the processional? Miss L.G., Pittsburgh, Pennsylvania**

I would prefer to see you have a maid or matron of honor as well as a junior bridesmaid. Such a young girl might feel nervous acting as your only attendant. However, if you feel that she can do it, she walks directly in front of you. If you decide to have a maid or matron of honor as well, the junior bridesmaid precedes the bridesmaid.

✝   ✝   ✝

**My daughter is to be married soon, and we are considering how large a wedding we can afford. Could you give me some idea of the expenses involved for both the bride and the groom? Mrs. R.W., Detroit, Michigan**

Traditionally the bride's parents assume the following expenses:

Engraved invitations and announcements
The bridal outfit and, if money is no object, the costumes of the bride's attendants (this is no longer expected)
Bridal photographs, bridal consultant, and social secretary, if needed
The bride's trousseau, including her household trousseau

All the cost of the reception, including the flowers for it

Flowers for the bride and her attendants (see "Groom's Expenses")

Music at the church and at the reception

Sexton's, organist's fee, and choir fee

Carpets, ribbons, awnings, tents—anything of the kind often rented for large weddings and receptions

Limousine for the bride, at least, and other cars for the transportation of the bridal party to and from church

A wedding gift of substance, usually silver

The groom assumes the following expenses:

The wedding ring

The marriage license

The bride's flowers (see note)

His own and the ushers' boutonnieres

Corsage for his mother

The ushers' gloves and ties

Gifts for the ushers

The minister's fee

A wedding gift for his bride—something for her to treasure, usually jewelry

His bachelor dinner

The entire cost of the wedding trip

His own wedding and wedding trip clothes

The home into which they will move and the equipping of it with its major furnishings

NOTE  In large formal weddings the bride's flowers and those of the bridesmaids are considered part of the entire wedding expense and thus borne by the bride's parents. It is becoming customary however for the groom to send the bride's bouquet, though she selects it, and to provide his own, the best man's, his father's, and the ushers' boutonnieres. In some communities the groom pays for the entire bridal party flowers as well as for corsages for both mothers. Sometimes the mothers and the grandmothers decide not to wear corsages.

*✦ ✦ ✦*

When my husband and I were married, almost five years ago, we did not have a double ring ceremony. Now he has expressed the wish to have one, providing it would be good taste to start wearing one at this later date. Would this be proper? Certainly I would very much like to give him one. And if it would be all right, should I just present it to him as a gift or should we arrange for some sort of church ceremony (Episcopal) for his putting it on? Mrs. R.L.T., Salt Lake City, Utah

As you know, in the Episcopal service there is a blessing of the ring. So you may take the ring to church and, by pre-arrangement with the rector, have it blessed. There is, too, a little publication called *The Book of Offices* (published by the Church Pension Fund, New York, N.Y.) which your rector undoubtedly has in his library. In it is a simple service designed for the blessing of married couples who have had only a civil ceremony. Within this service is the ceremony of the blessing of the ring, and perhaps your rector could adapt the service to a brief one for you for a reaffirmation of the marriage vows, with or without your friends as witnesses. I have long felt that churches would be wise to encourage couples to re-affirm their vows at stated times, perhaps on major anniversaries, in the church, and perhaps such reminders would help to hold marriages together. Certainly your husband's asking for a wedding band now, after five years of marriage, is a great tribute to you and to the institution of marriage itself.

✓ ✓ ✓

I was married in an Orthodox Jewish ceremony in which the marriage ring is placed on the right hand, as you know. My mother, who was born in Europe, objects to my removing the band and placing it on my left hand as is the custom in this country. She continues to wear hers on the fourth finger of the right hand. Don't you think I should conform to the American tradition in this case? Mrs. H.W., Los Angeles, California

Yes, it is usual for Jewish brides in this country to transfer the ring to the left hand. In our culture here the wedding band on the third finger of the left hand indicates a married woman. Worn on the right hand, the ring has no special significance here.

✓ ✓ ✓

My fiancé has asked me to go to a wedding with him, to which I wasn't invited. The wedding is his brother's sister-in-law. Would it be proper for me to attend it without a written invitation? "Troubled," Macon, Georgia

If the wedding is to be in church, you may go without an invitation. But you may not go to a reception following the wedding without an invitation, and as the wedding seems to be very soon, it would be unwise for your friend to ask for an invitation for you.

✓      ✓      ✓

My son has just returned home from overseas with a foreign bride. What is expected of me as to entertainment or a dinner so that relatives and friends may meet my new daughter-in-law? C.E.F., Spokane, Washington

You may give a tea or any other gathering that is convenient for you and invite to it relatives and friends who would be interested in meeting your daughter-in-law. You may invite them by telephone, by note, or by word of mouth, or by a combination of these. When people arrive, you and your daughter-in-law stand to greet them. You introduce young people to her and her to older people.

✓      ✓      ✓

There is to be a big wedding in our town, and the groom's father has been married twice, the first time to a very difficult alcoholic. The father and the first wife are very unfriendly and even a chance encounter usually causes fireworks. We know she will insist on coming to the wedding. Could we properly ask her not to? What is your solution? W.P.R., Meriden, Connecticut

Have some trusted member of the family, known for his tact, visit the mother and explain the situation. Say her son wants her to witness his wedding but that he does not want the occasion spoiled in any way. Say that someone (who can be trusted) will call for her and take her home immediately after the service. Alcoholics differ greatly, psychologically, but perhaps such an appeal to her pride and motherhood will help.

✓   ✓   ✓

**Is it proper to autograph wedding photographs when we send them to our friends and relatives?** D.C.C., Muncie, Indiana

Yes, but it isn't necessary.

## THE RECEPTION

**I am having a large reception following our wedding, and here is our problem. Some of the ushers are married, and I would like to know whether it is necessary to seat their wives with us at the bride's table. Will you also tell me who proposes the first toast to me?** D.A., West Orange, New Jersey

You need not include the mates of married attendants at the bridal table unless they are really strangers to the rest of the guests and would feel uncomfortable if left to their own devices. The best man rises and proposes the first toast to the bride and others follow suit—not forgetting to toast the groom, too. The bride, seated, may also propose a toast to the groom by turning her head toward him, lifting her glass, and smiling.

Here is a diagram of the bride's table.

THE BRIDE'S TABLE, *seating optional, see text. Reading from left to right:* Usher, bridesmaid, best man, bride, groom, maid or matron of honor, bridesmaid, usher.

✓   ✓   ✓

We are going to have a parents' table at our wedding reception but would like to know who sits where. Can you give me directions? U.C.M., St. Louis, Missouri

When a parents' table is provided, guests are placed as follows: father of the groom to the right of the bride's mother. Opposite her sits the bride's father with the groom's mother to the right. Other guests may include the clergyman and his wife. Here is the diagram.

SEATING AT PARENTS' TABLE, *table optional.* 1. Bride's mother, 2. father of groom, 3. father of bride, 4. mother of groom, 5. important officiating clergyman's wife, 6. officiating clergyman (*or see text*), 7, 8, 9, 10, 11, 12, 13, 14, friends of parents.

We are really an enormous family, close-knit and with many friends. One of us is going to be married, and we would like to be able to invite all our family and close friends to a reception as well as to the church. But to do this in the traditional way, with a caterer, would cost too much. Would it be all right if we hired a large hall with kitchen facilities and, more or less pitching in ourselves, preparing the day before the things that we would like to serve at our wedding dinner? We could hire waitresses to serve it. If we did this, what in the world would we serve, handling it this way? J.P., Broken Bow, Nebraska

Your solution is a good one. It is not necessary to have professional help at a wedding dinner or reception. You may well do all the work yourselves, and it isn't necessary either to have professional servers. I suggest that you prepare roasts of various kinds—beef, ham, turkey—and hearty salads, such as cooked vegetable salad or potato salad, with the usual relishes. You then handle it much as you would a church supper, letting people serve themselves from a buffet. Your wedding cake may be homemade or bakery made, and as a beverage you may serve anything from fruit punch or cider to champagne, as your pocketbook and tastes dictate.

✦ ✦ ✦

**My son is about to be married, and his future parents-in-law have asked us to keep down our guest list to approximately fifty for the reception. However, this number will not even cover the members of our own family. Could I ask her family's permission to submit a larger list so that I may include some intimate friends, agreeing to pay for all over fifty? Mrs. C.A.B., Concord, Massachusetts**

If you make your own guest list over fifty, offering to pay the difference, I think you may tend to make the bride's family feel uncomfortable. As you realize, the bride's family is responsible for the cost of the reception, and they could not properly accept your offer to pay for additional guests.

✦ ✦ ✦

**In the cutting of the wedding cake, where does the bride stand? L.C.N., Shreveport, Louisiana**

The bride stands to the groom's right. She places her hand on the cake knife, and he places his right hand over hers for the cutting of the first slice.

✦ ✦ ✦

**At the reception, does the bride's father dance first with his own wife or with the mother of the groom? Does he wait until all the guests have started dancing to do this? J.K., Estes Park, Colorado**

Dancing begins after the bride and groom have had the first dance —usually a waltz—alone on the dance floor together. Then the bride's father leads out the mother of the groom, and the groom's father dances with the mother of the bride. Attendants join in, and finally the guests enter the dance floor as they desire.

After the initial dance with the groom, the bride is claimed by her father-in-law, and the groom dances with his mother-in-law before asking the bridesmaids. The bride then dances with her father, next with the best man, and then with each of the ushers.

✔       ✔       ✔

**At a reception, must the guests stay to see the bride off or do they leave sooner?** E.F., Queens Village, Long Island

Just before leaving to dress for going away, the bride throws her bouquet to the bridesmaids. Dancing may continue, but usually it begins to come to a close and the guests start leaving. It is only the late-stayers who remain to see the bride off.

✔       ✔       ✔

**We are having a buffet reception after my wedding and do not plan to have a bride's table. After the groom and I receive, should we be seated for the collation or just stand around with the other guests, eating?** M.A., Boston, Massachusetts

Usually the bride and groom are seated alone at a small table for this first meal together after their marriage. They usually do not serve themselves but are waited upon from the buffet.

✔       ✔       ✔

**My sister, who is thirty-seven, will be married at a nuptial mass, and I will be her attendant. I am married and head of our family. At the reception should I be at the door receiving the guests with my gloves off or on, or does the bride come in later with her party when all are seated?** C.L.F., Buffalo, New York

Yes, you receive just inside the door as hostess for your sister, but the bridal party should arrive before the guests and form its receiving line beyond you at some focal point in the room. You keep your gloves on. The receiving line forms before the guests start arriving. Here is a diagram that will help you:

RECEIVING LINE AT WEDDING, *Optional Arrangement:* Bridal party before fireplace banked with flowers, or possibly in front of picture window.

1. Mother of bride, 2. father of groom (*optional*), 3. mother of groom (*optional*), 4. father of bride (*optional*), 5, 6. bridesmaids, 7. maid or matron of honor, 8. bride, 9. groom, 10. bridesmaid, 11. bridesmaid. NOTE: Whatever arrangement, the bride is on the groom's right except when he's in uniform. The best man is *never* on the line. Exceptions: Occasionally in the receiving line the bride must stand on the groom's left for convenience's sake. In this case the line must be routed so that the bride is reached first by the guests. If the groom's father acts as best man, he then may be in line.

I just received an invitation to attend a formal wedding. Please tell me the correct greeting to those in the receiving line. R.C., Lebanon, Pennsylvania

As the receiving line moves fairly swiftly, there is little time to say much. You may not have more than time to say, "How do you do" to the bride's mother, or, if she detains you, you can say anything nice and spontaneous you feel like saying. Remember that the reception is a social occasion, one for smiles and cheerful remarks. Just remember that you do not "congratulate" the bride. You "congratulate" the groom and "felicitate" the bride. To say anything like "Congratulations" to the bride is perhaps to indicate that you think she was lucky to find a husband at all! It is my theory that people don't really listen to what you say as you pass down the receiving line, so long as you look warm and gracious, pleased with the bride, and happy for the groom.

## ENTERTAINING BEFORE THE WEDDING

As I am getting married soon, I want to give a bachelor dinner. However, here in Chicago there have been some fashionable weddings where the bachelor dinner was given by the best man or by the ushers—in the latter case, "Dutch." Is this proper? If I give the dinner, where do I seat the best man? J.P.R., Chicago, Illinois

It is traditional for the groom to give the bachelor dinner, but, with the increasing simplification of weddings, very often the bachelor dinner doesn't take place at all anymore. However, it does usually take place before very large, formal weddings. I have never heard of its being given by other than the groom, but as we know, etiquette customs change and if in Chicago this one has, you may choose to follow the new custom or adhere to the old. If you give the dinner, you seat the best man to your right.

*✦ ✦ ✦*

Should I ask my house guests from out of town who are staying with me for the wedding to my wedding rehearsal dinner? S.A., Norfolk, Virginia

The rehearsal dinner is for the participants in the wedding. If those in your house party are not going to be in the wedding party itself, you need not include them, unless the rehearsal dinner is to be at your home and the guests for the house party have already arrived. Then it would be necessary to plan the party to include them.

## DRESS

### *Bride and Her Attendants*

With a bridal gown, what kind of shoes are worn and what kind of jewelry? When I go to the altar should I leave my engagement ring at home or wear it? P.C.O., Buffalo, New York

Bridal shoes are usually white silk or satin sandals or pumps. Jewelry should be limited to either that which is functional, such as a pin needed to hold the dress together, to a strand of pearls, perhaps small gold or pearl earrings. A watch or bracelet should not be worn. The engagement ring may be worn on the right hand or left at home until after the ceremony.

✓ ✓ ✓

**I am being married at home. Should I wear a hat and gloves? Is music necessary? Would I simply wait with the families until the ceremony begins?** L.M., Boston, Massachusetts

Yes, wear a hat or a substitute such as a Chanel bow unless your church does not require or request headcovering. Gloves are worn with the seam of the third finger, left hand, ripped so you may receive the ring easily. However, if a long-sleeved gown is worn, no gloves are required. Music is not necessary, but if you have a piano or a record player it is nice to have "The Wedding March," at least, played at the right moment. You stay upstairs or in another room until the ceremony begins, when you enter with your father or whoever is going to escort you to the altar.

✓ ✓ ✓

**My wedding is to be simple and small. It will be in our Episcopal church with no music and only a few close relatives. However, I would like to dress as a bride and have a large reception at our country club. Is this in proper taste?** Miss N.C.H., Duluth, Minnesota

Yes, you may have your church wedding witnessed by just a few and then have as large a reception as you wish. Of course, you may wear a wedding gown.

✓ ✓ ✓

**I am being married at home soon. I am thirty-five. Is beige antique silk, short length, all right, or would a coffee color be smarter? I don't want to look like an old girl trying to look young. Beige is becoming. My mother is trying to hold out for white with all the trimmings. Please try to help me convince her to the contrary.** Miss D.W., Dallas, Texas

Explain to your mother that while you are a very young thirty-five and would probably look fetching in a bridal gown with veil, this youthful costume might not be flattering to the contemporaries who will act as your attendants. While you have a perfect right to wear a wedding veil, I believe your decision not to is better. Wear either beige or coffee, short or long, whichever you prefer, but at thirty-five don't try to be a blushing bride, no matter what your mother tells you.

✓    ✓    ✓

**I'd like to have my bridesmaids dressed exactly alike. Is this correct? What about my maid of honor? V.C., New York, New York**

Yes, your bridesmaids' dresses may all be exactly alike, with different headdress and/or slightly different dress distinguishing the maid of honor. All their dresses should be the same length as the bride's, and they may wear flower headdresses, hats, or Juliet caps. The bridesmaids' slippers are all alike, but the maid or matron of honor may have slippers to match her dress. In the formal wedding party, only the bride may be gloveless (if her sleeves are long).

## Groom, Best Man and Ushers

**We are getting married at a formal daytime wedding at high noon. I am wearing a formal wedding gown. Is it all right if the groom wears a director's jacket with striped trousers instead of a cutaway which he thinks is unbecoming to him because he isn't very tall—five feet, eight. D.P.A., Phoenix, Arizona**

Yes, if he wishes, he may wear the director's jacket (a double-breasted sack coat), which is now also considered formal daytime wear. He wears it with striped trousers, gray vest, wing collar and black-and-white ascot or cravat, black shoes, and a black Homburg if he prefers, rather than the high silk hat traditional with the cutaway. At a late spring wedding or in summer, ushers in morning coats (either the cutaway or the director's jacket) frequently go hatless, but they may also wear straw or panama hats.

✓    ✓    ✓

I am not going to have a really formal daytime wedding as I am planning on only one attendant, and my marriage will take place at home. I am going to wear a veil, and my fiancé is worried about what he should wear. H.E.H., Winnetka, Illinois

The groom wears a single- or double-breasted Oxford gray coat, striped trousers, white shirt, stiff collar, gray tie, black shoes and socks, black or gray felt hat.

Is it proper for me to wear a director's jacket and striped trousers and spats at my afternoon wedding to a divorcée who will wear a dressy silk suit? R.M.H., Las Vegas, Nevada

Yes, but the spats may be omitted. A London friend of mine who is dressed by Bond Street tells me spats are never seen anymore over there at the most formal weddings. And even in this country I find they are not readily obtainable so must be a dying fashion.

At a formal daytime wedding, must all the ushers and the best man be dressed alike? And what if one of the ushers is in the armed services? G.L., New Haven, Connecticut

The rule here is that if the groom and his best man wear dark clothes, the ushers don't wear, for example, white linen suits, as there must be unity in the wedding party. However, today, sometimes the ushers will wear director's jackets and striped trousers, while the groom and best man wear the cutaway, which is the more formal daytime dress. A member of the armed services, acting as an usher or an attendant, wears his uniform, or, if regulations permit and he so desires, he wears the same civilian clothes as the others. A uniform of the armed forces is considered perfectly formal and appropriate for all social occasions.

Should the male members of a formal wedding wear white handkerchiefs in their breast pockets? If so, how should these be arranged? T.O'C., Nashville, Tennessee

A handkerchief in the breast pocket of a man's suit is always a finishing touch. White handkerchiefs are always correct for any formal occasion, although they may have monograms in black, white, gray, or maroon. A man's handkerchief is usually shaken out and then put casually in his pocket, not arranged in little points. The square fold is equally acceptable, though probably not as popular.

✓    ✓    ✓

My fiancé's wish is to wear his uniform at the wedding. He is in the Army. I would like to know what the best man and the groom's father should wear. It will be a morning wedding and I will be wearing a semi-formal gown. S.H., Oakland, California

The best man and the groom's father should wear dark business suits, white shirts, conservative ties, dark socks, black shoes.

## Parents of the Bride and Groom

My daughter is getting married in June and has planned what she is going to wear and what her attendants will wear but has no idea of what her mother and I should wear. The wedding is going to take place at four in the afternoon. "Father," Toledo, Ohio

The fathers of the bride and groom dress as the groom does. The mothers of the bride and groom wear soft suits or afternoon dresses in pale or pastel colors for a wedding at this hour. Guests at such a wedding wear the sort of clothes that they would wear to any formal afternoon function.

✓    ✓    ✓

We are having a formal evening wedding. My groom will wear white tie and so will his best man. Is it all right if the ushers wear white dinner jackets, as the wedding will take place in July? Miss B.S., Charleston, South Carolina

I suggest that the groom, his best man, and the fathers involved all wear white dinner jackets and abandon the idea of tails this late in the season. It would not be correct for the ushers to be dressed so differently from the principals.

✓　　✓　　✓

**My daughter is being married at home with a reception following. Is a taffeta dress and small, matching dressy hat all right for me to wear? Must I wear the hat all during the reception or should I keep it on just during the religious ceremony? The reception will go on all evening. Mrs. M.C., Jefferson, Georgia**

The costume you describe is quite all right. It is necessary to wear the hat only during the religious ceremony—just as if you were in church (if it is an Episcopal ceremony or, unlikely at home, a Catholic one). You may, if you wish, remove it later.

✓　　✓　　✓

**My daughter is being married in church at 7:30 P.M. There is a difference of opinion as to whether I must wear a hat and gloves. A reception will follow at a hall. Must I wear a hat and gloves during the whole evening? Mrs. F.M., Chicago, Illinois**

You should wear your hat (if the ceremony is Episcopal or Roman Catholic) and gloves at the church, although you may substitute a flower headdress or veil, if you wish. You may remove both of these for the reception, once the receiving line has broken up.

## Guests

**I am invited to a Sunday wedding at 12:30 P.M. Should I wear a cocktail dress or something less formal, such as a suit? Is a hat necessary? Mrs. R.K.L., Pittsburgh, Pennsylvania**

As this is probably a dressy occasion and the wedding followed by a reception, a dress would be more suitable unless you have a very dressy type of suit, say in velvet, faille, or slipper satin. You should wear a hat or a veil.

✓　　✓　　✓

**Everyone writes so much about the bride's clothes, but who gives any thought for what guests at an informal daytime wedding**

should wear? I am never sure whether I am dressed up enough or overdressed. Is there some rule about it? Mrs. L.J., Richmond, Virginia

The best rule is that at informal weddings guests wear conservative church-going clothes and that women wear hats, or hat substitutes, and gloves.

✓      ✓      ✓

I am invited to a Jewish wedding at a Conservative synagogue, and although I am not a Jew myself, I understand I am supposed to wear a hat. It happens that I rarely wear a hat, so if I should go without one, would I be wrong in following my own custom? N.B.B., El Paso, Texas

Yes, you would. It is proper for a man, on entering a Conservative synagogue, to take up one of the prayer caps, or yamalkes, available to you. Sometimes these are of paper and sometimes of fabric. You would also wear a yamalke in an Orthodox synagogue but not in a Reform one.

✓      ✓      ✓

I know when I go to a church wedding that if I am invited by the bride or know that I am indebted to her for the invitation —I say to the usher who comes to escort me, "Bride," and that he places me on the left in the pew reserved for the bride's guests and family. The groom's guests of course sit on the right—but I understand that this is different in Jewish synagogues. As I expect to go to a Jewish wedding soon, will you please set me right? R.K., Montgomery, Alabama

In Reform temples, the custom is the same as it is in churches— the bride's guests to the left, the bride's side of the church. However, in Orthodox and Conservative synagogues, the groom's guests receive the left-hand seats, the bride's the right.

✓      ✓      ✓

Would it be proper to wear a navy-blue sheer dress at a November wedding? The reception is in the afternoon. W.T.S., New Orleans, Louisiana

A navy sheer is a summer fabric. If you have something else that would be suitable, wear it.

⁋   ⁋   ⁋

Would it be all right for me to wear a suit to a five o'clock wedding? S.J.G., Harrisburg, Pennsylvania

Yes, if it is a soft, dressy one. Wear dressy shoes and an appropriate hat or hat substitute. A tailored suit would be inappropriate.

⁋   ⁋   ⁋

My nephew is getting married, and I am not to be in the wedding party, although I will be a guest. My daughter insists that I should not wear my best black dress—that black isn't proper at a wedding. I'd like to wear it and brighten it with a little pink. Would this be all right? C.C.A., Chicago, Illinois

Yes, you may wear the dress you describe, and brightening it with pink would make it more festive. It is only the women who are in the wedding party who may not wear black—guests may do so, of course, especially in big cities.

⁋   ⁋   ⁋

I am going to a large, formal wedding to be held at 8 P.M. in a hotel in a near-by city. I intend to wear a dark, street-length dress. Should my husband wear a dark suit or something more formal? Mrs. E.D., Charleston, South Carolina

It would be correct for your husband to wear a dinner jacket at the wedding you mention. However, if possible, check with others who are going to see what the men plan to wear. If other men guests plan to wear dark suits, your husband would prefer to dress as they do. If you know no one going but can find out what the groom is going to wear, that can help you decide. If he is going to be in tails, the male guests wear dinner jackets unless they are part of the bridal party, in which case they, too, wear tails.

⁋   ⁋   ⁋

Are a street-length dress, small hat, and white gloves suitable attire for a church wedding taking place at 6 P.M.? In a Protestant
church, is a hat necessary or out of place at that particular hour?
At the reception at a club, does one remove gloves and carry
them with purse or tuck them in purse? I do not wish to buy new
formal clothes and hope the cocktail-type outfit will be proper.
Jane A., Providence, Rhode Island

Yes, this is a suitable costume for a wedding at such a time. In
most Protestant churches women are expected to wear hats. In
Protestant Episcopal churches they are requested to do so. A hat
in church is never incorrect for a woman. At the reception you
may remove your gloves and carry them with your purse, once
refreshments have been served. You keep them on, however, as
you go down the receiving line.

## SECOND MARRIAGES

I expect to marry a widower (I am a widow) this year. He would
like to give me a diamond ring on my birthday in the spring.
Would this be proper? Would it be in good taste for my mother to
announce our engagement in the paper? We are both forty-three.
If this is not correct, how should it be done? We live in a small
community where we are well-known and plan a small, quiet
wedding in our church. Does this sound proper? A.F., Niagara
Falls, New York

Yes, your fiancé may give you an engagement ring. However,
such engagements are usually made known only informally among
one's friends and relatives rather than announced in the newspapers. You may issue news of the marriage jointly in the following manner:

> Mrs. Harry Holden, of 8 East 10th Street, and Mr. Rutherford
> Tyng, of Princeton, New Jersey, announce that their marriage
> took place Saturday, April 3d, at the Church of the Ascension,
> Baltimore, Maryland. Mrs. Holden, the former Elsbeth Finn,

is the daughter of Mr. and Mrs. Clarence Finn, of Baltimore. Mrs. Holden is the widow of the late Mr. Harry Holden, who died in 1963.

Mr. Tyng was married to the former Elizabeth Johnson of this city, who died last year. He is the son of Professor and Mrs. Rufus Tyng of Princeton and is an instructor in mathematics at Princeton University. The couple will make their home in Philadelphia.

✓ ✓ ✓

**I am marrying a widower. Is it correct for me to wear a wedding gown and veil? K.D.W., Eugene, Oregon**

Yes, indeed. The status of the groom has nothing to do with the matter. The bride who has never been married before may wear the wedding veil, although if she has reached her mid-thirties or more she usually prefers not to, no matter how youthful she may look.

✓ ✓ ✓

**I am a widow and am getting married again. I understand it is not correct for me to wear anything that looks like a wedding dress even at a church wedding, which is where I am getting married. I am going to wear a pale gray silk suit and a pink flowered hat and will wear a corsage of sweetheart roses. What should my groom wear? T.G., Cleveland, Ohio**

When the bride does not wear a veil, the groom wears a dark blue or gray business suit, white shirt with fold collar, conservative tie, a derby or Homburg, and gray gloves. If the wedding is to take place in summer, he may wear a light-weight wool suit in gray or blue with white shirt and black shoes, or a Palm Beach suit, conservative tie, white shirt, black socks, and black shoes. In the country, he may wear a navy jacket and white flannel trousers, white shirt, black socks, conservative tie, and black shoes. Optionally, he may wear navy or charcoal silk jacket and oxford trousers or possibly a raw silk suit in natural, navy, or oxford.

✓ ✓ ✓

I am a widower. I plan to marry a widow. We are prominent, and our wedding will be covered by the newspapers. In furnishing them with information, must I necessarily state the name of my former wife? This is complicated, as before I became a widower I was divorced, and I would rather skip the whole matter. Mr. W.L.B., Philadelphia, Pennsylvania

The press release may read merely, "was married to Mr. John Benson Jones." Sometimes, when people are very prominent, there is what is called a "morgue" or newspaper file on them, into which society editors dip when anything of consequence takes place concerning them. When this possibility exists, it is usually a good idea to furnish the information, but in this case it would not be necessary to mention the prior divorce. You could, however, have a line such as, "Mr. Jones was married previously to the late Anita Lawrence Payne (adding, optionally, from whom he was divorced).

✓    ✓    ✓

I would like to know if it is good taste for a divorcée to be the honoree at one or more small parties before her second marriage. She did not live in this area during her first marriage, and her prospective bridegroom was not previously married. L.P.B., Seattle, Washington

I see no reason why she couldn't have some parties given for her so long as they are not showers. Showers are not usually given for second marriages.

✓    ✓    ✓

For a second marriage is it permissible for me to have a close relative (matron of honor) to stand with me and for the groom to have an attendant? What kind of invitation, if any, should I use? K.R., Macon, Georgia

You may have a close relative as a matron of honor and your husband-to-be may have a close friend as his best man who both, incidentally, may act as your witnesses. As both of you usually must have witnesses—adult ones—it is nicer if they are close friends or relatives rather than strangers. (For example, at a civil wedding in a courthouse or elsewhere any adult witnesses are often used, whether or not they know the bride and groom.) This is also the case when a couple goes alone for a quiet ceremony in a church or in the vestry.

✓     ✓     ✓

I am a young widow and I am planning to get married again in the fall. Naturally I have a great many household things from my previous marriage, many of which were wedding gifts. I am wondering if it is proper to specify, on wedding invitations, that it is to be a "purse wedding." If so, how is it done? F.A.B., Greenwich, Connecticut

Formal invitations are usually not sent for second marriages. And you wouldn't engrave on an invitation any such information as you would like to impart. You can let it be known through close friends and your family that you would prefer gifts of money from those close to you. However, quite often those friends who have sent gifts for a first marriage do not do so for a second and should not really be expected to do so.

## INVITATIONS, ANNOUNCEMENTS, AND REPLIES

What is the traditional form for formal wedding invitations and when should they be sent out? Miss L.M., Houston, Texas

Wedding invitations are sent four weeks in advance. Here is an example:

*Dr. and Mrs. Grant Kingsley*
*request the honour of your presence*
*at the marriage of their daughter*
*Penelope*
*to*
*Mr. George Frank Carpenter*
*on Friday, the tenth of June*
*one thousand nine hundred and sixty-seven*
*at twelve o'clock*
*Saint Mary's Church*
*San Francisco*

Mention of the year is optional on an invitation but obligatory on the announcement of the marriage. The word "honour" is always spelled in the old way. The phrase "honour of your presence" is always used for invitations to the church. When the marriage takes place at home or somewhere other than church, the phrase "pleasure of your company" is used. No R.S.V.P. is used where the invitation is for the ceremony alone. The R.S.V.P. is used only on the reception cards, if any.

✓    ✓    ✓

**What is the proper location for a zip code when writing an address? Should zip codes be used when addressing wedding invitations?** Mrs. I.R., Freeport, New York

Zip codes should now be used whenever you write an address—even on wedding invitations. They are placed immediately following the state with no punctuation in between. Here is an example:

> *Mrs. Robert S. Miller*
> *19 Barclay Street*
> *Douglaston, New York 11363*

✓    ✓    ✓

**My daughter plans to be married in the church by the priest and at the altar. However, only the families of the bride and groom will attend, and there will be no reception afterward, just a small dinner party. Is it proper for us to send wedding announcements? Should they be sent out before or after the marriage? Could you give me some kind of form so I could have them made up?** Mrs. C.S.T., Fort Worth, Texas

Yes, send out the announcements immediately after the wedding. They should be ordered a month to six weeks before the wedding and should be all addressed, ready for mailing, as soon as the ceremony has taken place. Here is the form:

*Dr. and Mrs. Grant Kingsley*
*have the honour of announcing*
*(or have the honour to announce)*
*the marriage of their daughter*
*Penelope*
*to*
*Mr. George Frank Carpenter*
*on Friday, the ninth of June*
*one thousand nine hundred and sixty-seven*
*(must give year)*
*Saint Mary's Church*
*(optional to mention)*
*San Francisco*

✱   ✱   ✱

I have been on my own for many years and have no close relatives or friends to issue my invitations and announcements for me. May I do this myself? A.L.C., Los Angeles, California

Yes you may, and quite properly too. Here is the form you would use:

*The honour of your presence*
*is requested at the marriage of*
*(or "wedding reception of")*
*Miss Cordelia Kingsley*
*(note "Miss")*
*to*
*(or "and")*
*Mr. Winthrop Cass Bowers*
*etc.*

Your announcement would read:

*Miss Cordelia Kingsley (note "Miss")*
*and*
*Mr. Winthrop Cass Bowers*
*announce their marriage*
*at the Church of All Saints (optional)*
*at Greenwich, Connecticut*
*on Tuesday, the seventh of March*
*one thousand nine hundred and sixty-seven*

✱   ✱   ✱

I am having a large church wedding with a reception following, to which I plan to invite about a hundred guests. Could you give me the proper form for the reception card? R.N., Albany, New York

When not all those attending the wedding are to be invited to the reception, a reception card of the same stock as the invitation and about half the size is included with its tissue. It should not bear a crest, shield, or motto and may read:

*Dr. and Mrs. Grant Kingsley*
*request the pleasure of your company*
*at the wedding breakfast*
*following the ceremony*
*at*
*"The Gulls"*
*Belvedere*
*R.S.V.P. (or "The favor of a reply is requested")*

Note "pleasure of your company," as this is now a social occasion.

✓    ✓    ✓

**Should the tissues that come with engraved invitations from the stationer's be left in place when the invitations are placed in the inner envelope, or should they be removed? L.P., Hartford, Connecticut**

Unless they have been ordered very far in advance so that you are sure the ink is well dried, it is safest and usual to leave the tissue in place.

✓    ✓    ✓

**Is it necessary to reply to a wedding invitation? What is the correct form? Miss L.B., Wichita, Kansas**

Formal, engraved invitations to a church wedding do not require answering. But if a reception card is received, one answers in the traditional form in response to the R.S.V.P. on the invitation. The reply is written in longhand on one's best conservative paper in blue or black ink, with the wording and spacing taking the form of engraving.

> *Mr. and Mrs. Morrow Tuft*
> *accept with pleasure*
> *Dr. and Mrs. Kingsley's*
> *kind invitation for*
> *Friday, the ninth of June*
> *at noon*

A regret follows the same form. It reads:

> *Mr. and Mrs. Morrow Tuft*
> *regret that they are unable to accept*
> *Dr. and Mrs. Kingsley's*
> *etc.*

On a regret, the repetition of the time is unnecessary.

✔  ✔  ✔

**I am sending out formal invitations to my forthcoming wedding. Are there any rules about the addressing of envelopes that should be adhered to? K.R., Akron, Ohio**

Yes, the addressing of wedding invitations and announcements is rigidly prescribed. Black ink must be used. Abbreviations are not permitted except in "Dr.," "Mr.," "Mrs.," and "Jr." (or "Lt." when combined with "Colonel," etc.). The names of cities and states are written out. And use the zip code when there is one. For instance:

> *Mr. and Mrs. Cedric Moore McIntosh*
> *1886 Shore Road*
> *Chicago, Illinois 60600*

Where there are several members of a family to be invited, avoid the phrase "and family." On the inside envelope is written:

> *Mr. and Mrs. McIntosh*
> *(no Christian name)*
> *Belinda and Gordon*
> *(if the children are under age)*

If there are other adults in the family whom you wish to invite, they must receive separate invitations.

It is also traditional for the handwriting (in black ink) on the envelopes to be obviously feminine and, if possible, of a round, clear style. The address, of course, may never be typed.

✁ ✁ ✁

I am planning an informal, morning church wedding to be followed by a wedding breakfast. Most of the groom's relatives and friends live in a city considerably distant from this. It is likely that only one or two will attend the ceremony. We would like to know whether it is necessary to send wedding invitations to relatives at such a distance and whether close friends who we know can't attend should receive invitations. Miss A.S., Springfield, Illinois

Send invitations to all relatives and to close friends even if you know they cannot attend. To friends who do not receive invitations, send announcements.

✁ ✁ ✁

In addressing wedding invitations, how do you address the envelope to two sisters, both single? K.V.C., San Jose, California

Address them "The Misses Clark," both on the outer and on the inner envelope.

✁ ✁ ✁

I am having a small informal wedding. Do I send out engraved invitations? R.C.M., Galveston, Texas

No. This type of wedding does not call for formal invitations. Invitations can be extended either by telephone or by short informal notes to your friends. However, announcements usually are sent after the wedding to as large a list of friends, relatives, and acquaintances as you care to cover.

✁ ✁ ✁

I would like to have my wedding invitations engraved in gold ink. Is this correct? What color stationery do you recommend? A.F., Akron, Ohio

For wedding invitations, only black ink should be used. Silver or gold inks are frequently used however for the twenty-fifth or fiftieth wedding anniversary invitations if one wishes. The most distinguished wedding paper is the traditional ivory or ecru, but pure white is frequently used, too. I feel that the icy blue and pale pink papers sometimes offered—and by good stationers, too—do get away too radically from the traditional bridal white or ivory.

*  *  *

I work for a large company where I'm not personally acquainted with all the employees and have only a speaking acquaintance with others. Of course, I know those with whom I work each day very well. Would it be permissible for me to send one wedding invitation to be placed on the bulletin board, or should I send invitations only to those I think would like to come? Some girls I know have sent just one invitation in the past, and those in the company who wanted to attend went and vice versa. N.W., Bangor, Maine

I would send an invitation to those with whom you have a warm social bond in business—if such is the case—and I see no reason why you cannot send your wedding invitation for the bulletin board for others who might know you slightly and wish to see you married—if, of course, your wedding is to take place in a church.

*  *  *

My daughter eloped—with our approval, I may add—but should we send formal announcements or leave them out and just tell our friends about the marriage? Mrs. W.B., Houston, Texas

It is not necessary that you send them, although you may. If you do send them, state the place of the marriage and the date. If a civil ceremony was performed, only the name of the city or town appears. If the couple was married in church, it is optional whether the church is mentioned or not.

*  *  *

Etiquette blithely ignores the fact that sometimes divorce isn't as final as it should be and could be, and that often the participants are in the somewhat uncertain position of wondering how they should tell their friends who are out of town (and certainly wouldn't know otherwise) that they have remarried. This isn't such an unusual situation after all. Of forty-one marriage licenses recently listed in our local paper, thirteen were remarriages of divorced couples. Please do let me know what to do. Mr. J.M.H., Hot Springs, Arkansas

The good news that two people have come together again despite divorce is proclaimed to their friends and relatives by telephone, telegram, and, of course, by note and word of mouth. Formal announcements are not sent out.

## GIFTS

**Is it expected that the bride put her wedding gifts on display?** O.M.E., Roanoke, Virginia

A formal display of wedding gifts is less often seen now, but it is still in good taste to exhibit them. Cards are now removed from the gifts displayed, and gifts of like value are grouped together. Checks are recorded on propped-up cards reading "Check, $100," with the donor's name *omitted*.

✔  ✔  ✔

**The people with whom I work will be unable to attend my wedding without loss of pay, since it is to be on a weekday. However, there are several close ones who should be invited. But does an invitation imply a wedding gift is expected? I do not want it to appear as such. J.T.B., Thomasville, Pennsylvania**

Invite your friends, even though you know they cannot attend. An invitation to a wedding does not obligate anyone to send a gift if the wedding is at church. Wedding guests included in the reception usually do send gifts if they accept and even when they regret, if they feel particularly close to the principals.

✔  ✔  ✔

In sending a check as a wedding gift, to whom is the check drawn—bride or groom or both? The check will be sent before the day of the wedding. R.C.H., Chicago, Illinois

Before the wedding, a check is drawn to the bride in her maiden name. A check presented by some member of the family after the wedding has taken place, perhaps just before the reception, is properly made out to the bride and groom, "Mr. and Mrs. Richard Brown," or "Anne and Richard Brown." But the use of "Mr. and Mrs." on their wedding check usually gives them a great thrill, for it is perhaps the bride's first use of her new name.

✓ ✓ ✓

Is it all right to use informals in giving thanks for a wedding present? B.G., New York, New York

Yes, so long as there is no printed phrase such as "Thank you" that substitutes for the written words of thanks and if the informal is conservative and of good quality paper. It should be sent, of course, first-class mail, sealed.

✓ ✓ ✓

I am leaving immediately after my wedding for six months abroad, where my husband is stationed. I am thanking as many people as possible before my wedding for gifts they have already sent. But I won't be able to see the gifts that arrive after my departure, and they won't be sent on to me. Shall I wait until I get back to thank the senders, or may my family handle the acknowledgments for me? Marilyn L., Atlanta, Georgia

There is a card available now at all good stationers who do wedding invitations and announcements. It may be used under the circumstances you describe or where there has been a very large formal wedding where hundreds of gifts have been received. It is sent immediately on receipt of the gift and merely states that Miss So-and-so has received your gift and will acknowledge it personally at an early date. In your case, your family should send you a list of the gifts that have arrived after the wedding so that you can make each note quite personal and appreciative.

✓ ✓ ✓

When I write my thank-you notes to my husband's relations, should I write "Dear Aunt Sally," etc., even when I haven't met them? My husband is very close to his family. K.V.C., Santa Barbara, California

Yes, address them as "Dear Aunt Sally," etc. They are now *your* relatives, too. Try to make your letter spontaneous and friendly, just as though you were talking face to face to the person who has sent you the gift. Thank-you notes are signed, "Sincerely," "Cordially," "Love," or "Affectionately."

✓    ✓    ✓

We find that brides are more and more using Mr. and Mrs. informals in giving thanks for wedding presents. We feel that this is not correct and wonder what your opinion is? Stationer, Rochester, New York

It would be awkward for a bride to use the Mr. and Mrs. informals in giving thanks for wedding presents. This piece of stationery is designed for the issuing of invitations and for inclusion with flowers or other gifts with an unsigned line or two—"A happy birthday!" "We hope you like it!" To use it for notes means that it has to be written in the second person plural and be signed by both people, an awkward procedure. Properly, the bride writes her own acknowledgment, and if she wishes to mention her husband in it—as is usually done—that is, of course, all right. But she should not sign the note jointly with her husband, or even as some girls do "Sincerely, Pat and Bill."

✓    ✓    ✓

Recently I gave a very nice wedding present to a young girl of whom I was very fond. The acknowledgment was so long in coming that I finally had to write her to ask if she had received my gift. After an even further delay she wrote that of course she had and that she and her husband were very pleased with it. Can't you say something about the necessity for prompt acknowledgment of wedding gifts? Mrs. L.V., Westport, Connecticut

Yes, a bride should acknowledge her wedding gifts as soon as possible, if only with a few lines. Where a great many gifts have been received and the bride is a working girl, this is very difficult, I know, but nevertheless it is a prime social obligation.

✓ ✓ ✓

Could you give me suggestions for suitable gifts for my brides-maids and also some ideas on what my fiancé can give his ushers? Are there any special rules? W.S.B., Essex, Connecticut

The only important rule is that the gifts be something that will be lasting mementos of the occasion. The gifts are usually silver or gold, engraved with the date and the initials of the recipient. The usher's gifts—cuff links, key rings, silver ash trays, bill clips—should be all alike, as are those of the bridesmaids. The chief attendants receive the same kind of gifts—bracelets, charms, com-pacts (usually something to wear or carry)—but they vary a little in design and size to give a little more importance to the chief attendants' gifts.

✓ ✓ ✓

My daughter recently married a service man at a registry office. Her father and I sent out announcements and "at home" cards to relatives and friends. Within a matter of weeks the couple have separated and have started suit for divorce. What should my daughter do about the gifts she has received and is still receiving? What do I do about those friends who inquire about my daughter and ask for gift suggestions? Must I explain that divorce is pending? I feel this is much too personal a problem to discuss, and frankly I'm not up to it. Mrs. H.E.K., Asheville, Kentucky

Your daughter is quite entitled to the gifts she has received and needn't worry about the necessity for returning them. Wedding gifts are returned only if the marriage is called off. She should send the usual thank-you note, without explanation of her problem, to those who send gifts. You can handle the situation on your end as delicately as possible by explaining that, as your daughter mar-ried a service man, her plans are rather indefinite and that she would prefer to wait before receiving anymore gifts. I think that you show great sensitivity in not discussing the difficult problem you all face. Even when a situation has become so drastic that divorce proceedings have been started, there is always the hopeful possibility of reconciliation. Those around them should give the couple every chance to come together again. Try to get your daughter and her husband to seek professional aid, if possible, to save their marriage.

## ANNIVERSARIES

**What do you consider the major wedding anniversaries and what are the proper gifts for them?** N.A., Detroit, Michigan

I find that the most celebrated wedding anniversaries are the first (paper, plastics), the fifth (wood and decorative accessories for the home), the tenth (tin or aluminum), the twenty-fifth (silver), the fiftieth (gold) and the seventy-fifth (diamond or gold).

*   *   *

**When one receives an invitation to a golden wedding anniversary, must one send a gift? We have had several invitations during the past year and are elderly people with a small retirement income.** Mrs. R.N.W., Ann Arbor, Michigan

You are not obliged to send a gift under the circumstances, especially if you do not attend. If you do send a gift, you send something that is well within your means. If this cannot be done, write a warm letter of felicitation, send a telegram, or take yellow flowers from your garden or a potted plant you have grown (and gild the pot), or bake a batch of cookies with golden icing. No worth-while friend asks the price of the gift you give. And if you have given of yourself in loving labor such a gift is beyond monetary valuation.

# FUNERALS

## Dear Miss Vanderbilt:

### FLOWERS

Can you tell me exactly how to send flowers to a funeral? How do I sign my name and do I address the flowers to the deceased or to his family? A.F., New Orleans, Louisiana

When flowers are sent to a funeral a plain white card is attached with the name of the sender, "Miss Helen Murray" or "Mr. and Mrs. Frederick Wallace," or a visiting card (a husband-and-wife card) may be used with a line drawn through the names in the case of intimate friends, and the message, "Deepest sympathy from Jean and Hugh," written in ink. The envelope is simply addressed to:

*The funeral of Mr. Lawrence Karl Volkman*
*Silvan Funeral Home*
*Greenpoint*

✦ ✦ ✦

When the funeral is at home, is it correct to leave the name cards on flowers that have been sent and are banked against the casket? Mrs. E.B.C., Charlotte, North Carolina

No, usually these are taken off by some member of the family who records "spray of carnations from the Gordon Joneses," so that the family member who acknowledges the flowers may make a specific reference to what was sent. It is always proper, if anyone asks, to say from whom a particularly lovely floral offering has come.

✦ ✦ ✦

When a death notice reads "Please omit flowers," does this mean you should send flowers under no circumstances? If the death notice suggests sending a check to a charity, how do you let the family know? Mrs. R.M.H., Brooklyn, New York

When the death notice reads "Please omit flowers," this request should be scrupulously respected. At some Protestant funerals the family prefers that the casket have one floral offering—that of the family. They sometimes request privately or in the death notice that flowers be sent to hospitals. Flowers may then be sent to hospital wards "In memory of ——— from ———" and the family may be so notified by note or when the funeral call is made. It is a growing custom for close friends to send flowers sometime during the weeks following the funeral (except to Jews). The accompanying card should avoid reference to the bereavement. It may read: "Kindest thoughts from us all, Peggy and John." When a request that a check be sent to a charity is given, you send the check to the charity and write a note to the family without, however, specifying the amount you have given. The charity notifies the bereaved family.

✓   ✓   ✓

I recently received a printed acknowledgment card for flowers which I had sent to the funeral of a friend. Are these printed acknowledgments replacing the handwritten note? F.L.M., Memphis, Tennessee

Morticians usually supply as part of their service printed acknowledgment cards to be sent out by the family. These should not be used instead of a handwritten note, however brief, although the use of personally engraved cards or folders for large funerals, where hundreds of letters and floral offerings are received, is quite understandable.

The note acknowledging flowers, a mass card (see page 110), charity contributions, or a telegram need not be more than a few words, such as:

Dear Mr. Scott,
You were kind indeed to think of us at such a difficult time. Your violets were beautiful and comforting.

Sincerely,<br>Helen Russell

## DRESS

**Do you feel it is essential for at least the family of the deceased to wear black at the funeral? And what about the children and the men?** B.M.F., Kansas City, Missouri

Black dresses from the regular wardrobe and in a dull material are usually worn by women members of the family at a funeral. Children wear Sunday school clothes in quiet colors or white. The black chiffon veil is often worn by the bereaved women at a funeral. Stockings are usually gun metal or black, but dark, neutral tones are worn too. Ordinary street clothes such as one would wear to church are acceptable for others attending a funeral. Men of the family wear cutaways for a large church funeral or dark business suits with black shoes and socks, black or gray ties, gray gloves, and white shirts.

## FUNERAL CALLS

**When a mortuary chapel is used, where does one make funeral calls? Must the family be represented at home as well as in the funeral chapel in order to receive calls?** R.McQ., Tucson, Arizona

Now that the mortuary chapel has so much replaced the home in the laying out of the dead, people are often confused as to where they are expected to make their funeral calls. If they are close friends or relatives they may call both at home and at the chapel if they wish, leaving their cards or signing the register at the funeral chapel. If calls are received at the funeral chapel some family representative should be present at least during the afternoon and early evening, when calls are likely to be made.

✔    ✔    ✔

Recently, having read the notice of the death of an old friend in the newspaper, I attended the funeral service. My daughter says it was incorrect for me to do this—that I should not have gone without an invitation. What is the etiquette in this case? Mrs. J.H., Red Bank, New Jersey

You were right. Unless the words "Funeral Private" appear in the death notice, any friend or acquaintance of the deceased or his family may attend the services, as do interested strangers if the funeral is in church. Close friends or relatives may ask the person in charge of arrangements for permission to attend the interment if they are able to provide their own transportation or if there seems to be adequate room in the funeral cars. They should be very certain that their presence at so difficult a time will be of real comfort to the immediate family, which usually prefers to be alone with the clergyman at the last brief rites.

✓    ✓    ✓

**Will you please tell me the correct signature for a married woman when signing the register in a funeral home under the following circumstances:**

1. If accompanied by husband, are both signatures signed on one line (like Mr. and Mrs.), or are they signed one beneath the other?

2. If husband and wife visit the funeral home at different hours (separately) does the earlier one visiting sign for the later one?

3. If a good friend of the deceased, does the married woman sign her own first name and her husband's last name? *P.S.F., Oakland, California*

1. They sign one line, "Mr. and Mrs. John Jones."

2. They sign for themselves separately as "Mrs. John Jones" and "John Jones."

3. She signs her proper title, "Mrs. John Jones," the reason being that after these signatures have been seen by the family, the visits may be acknowledged by someone—a social secretary or friend—who might not know that "Clara Jones" is properly addressed "Mrs. John Jones."

## PRESS NOTICES

**How is a paid death notice inserted in newspapers? And who does it?** O.T., New Orleans, Louisiana

The person in charge of the funeral prepares the death notices and may insert them himself in the local paper or have the mortician do so. A paid death notice may be phoned to papers selected, but it should always be *read* from carefully checked information. Where it is given over the phone, the newspaper's classified department usually calls back for recheck, to be certain the notice is legitimate. The form is:

> Volkman—Lawrence Karl, on November 23 (year optional), husband (or beloved husband) of Helen Schroeder Volkman (his wife's maiden name is always given to aid identification) and father of Louise and Peter Schroeder Volkman (the daughters are listed first). Funeral at (name of church and address, if necessary), at 2 P.M., Tuesday.

Sometimes, especially when there was no generally known preliminary illness, the word "suddenly" may be added after the names of the immediate family. If a man was married his wife is always listed first, not his parents, whose names, in this case, usually do not appear in the paid notice but who are mentioned, of course, in news stories.

## LETTERS OF CONDOLENCE AND REPLY

**How do you address a sympathy card to the married daughters and sons when the mother dies? Is it proper to sign it "Mr. and Mrs. Bowen and family"? A.S.M., Highland Park, Michigan**

You address not a sympathy card but a personal letter to the eldest daughter, who is now technically the female head of the family. In the letter, you refer in some way to the others. If a married couple is extending its sympathy, it is the wife who writes and in the body of the letter refers to the sympathy also extended by the husband. It is she who signs the letter. She does not sign it "Mary and John."

Social letters of condolence, always handwritten on conservative paper, need not be long. In fact, "Deepest sympathy" may be written on your visiting card in black ink. You always address your letter to the nearest relative, whether or not you are acquainted. It is better to avoid the words "died," "death," and "killed" in such letters. It is quite possible to write the kind of letter that will give a moment of courage and a strong feeling of sympathy without mentioning death or sadness at all. For instance:

Dear Jeanette:
It is several years since I have seen Larry, but it was with a real sense of loss that I heard the news. He will always be with us in spirit.

Most sincerely,<br>Mary

≁ ≁ ≁

**The death of a loved one occurred in our family a short time ago. Different members of the family have received numerous letters, notes, and cards of condolence. Should these be acknowledged by us? J.J.M., Hempstead, New York**

Those members of the family who have received letters of condolence answer them. Cards of condolence are not properly sent but if received may be acknowledged verbally or by personal notes on personally engraved cards or folders, if they are used.

In reply one may write at any length one wishes, but it is quite understandable that the note be brief, even to a close friend. Today it is usually on plain white paper. Black-bordered mourning paper is much less used now and quite unnecessary.

## CUSTOMS OF DIFFERENT FAITHS

**May a non-Catholic arrange for a mass card to be sent to a bereaved Catholic family? May he have a mass said for a Catholic friend who is ill? If so, how is this done? A.M., Des Moines, Iowa**

Yes, this may be done by anyone. The person who wishes the mass said calls upon any Catholic priest, either in his friend's parish or one in his own locality. He asks that the mass be said and he sometimes indicates the exact time he wishes it celebrated. The priest then gives the mass card to the donor, who may send it to the family or deliver it when making a funeral call. These masses may be arranged, too, for a year after the death, on its anniversary, or any time immediately after death has taken place. Recovery masses are often said for Catholics who are ill or facing operations. In this instance, a mass card may be taken by the donor to home or hospital when the sick call is being made. The person who arranges the mass makes a voluntary contribution to the church in which the mass is said—the amount varying, according to his own particular circumstances, from $1.00 to $5.00 and more.

✓    ✓    ✓

**Should a Protestant send flowers to an Orthodox Jewish funeral?
J.A., Louisville, Kentucky**

No. To Orthodox Jews flowers are a sign of joy—they should never be sent to a funeral. Often, too, flowers are not desired at a Conservative or Reform funeral.

✓    ✓    ✓

**I sometimes see Catholic funerals with masses of flowers in the cortege—although I understand it isn't customary for other than the family's flowers to be allowed in the church at a Catholic funeral. Is this correct? M.J.W., Montclair, New Jersey**

Many Catholics seem to prefer mass cards (see above) to flowers. In some Catholic parishes only the family's flowers are permitted in the church, although, of course, other flowers may be sent to the home or funeral home and be taken to the cemetery.

## SPECIAL PROBLEMS

**Please tell me what the correct name is for the grave marker of a widow. For example, Mary Elizabeth Smith married George Dwight Reilly. When she passes on, does her grave marker read: Mary S. Reilly or Mary E. Reilly? Mrs. I.J.P., Minot, North Dakota**

There is no very definite rule about this, and it is done both ways, either with the baptismal name—Mary Elizabeth—or with the maiden name, Mary Smith, combined with Reilly, her married name. However, my preference and that of top church authorities

I have discussed this with is for the retention of the maiden name for the sake of clearer family records. Therefore, it seems preferable for the marker to read Mary Smith Reilly.

ℐ      ℐ      ℐ

**When you have been invited to attend a funeral in a friend's family what is the proper reply? Mrs. S.F., Waterville, Maine**

You say, "Thank you for telling me. I shall be there." You obviously avoid any phrase that makes your acceptance sound like one to a social occasion. You cannot be "happy" to attend a funeral.

ℐ      ℐ      ℐ

**When a funeral service is held in church, does the minister receive a fee? Is this taken care of by the funeral director or the family? J.K.T., Columbus, Ohio**

It is usual (but not universal) for the minister to be given an honorarium for his services. Sometimes an appropriate amount is sent to him by the funeral director, who includes this expense on his bill. More often it is sent by a member of the family in a letter of appreciation for his comfort and help.

The amount should be based on the family's ability to make a contribution. Simplicity of the funeral is today no indication of lack of funds. Certainly if the funeral has been large and expensive the clergyman should not receive less than seventy-five to one hundred dollars. From the average family he usually receives from five to twenty-five dollars. Checks should be made out to the clergyman rather than to the church, as these fees are expected to contribute to his own expenses.

The sexton in a large church is on the church payroll and devotes full time to church business affairs. He receives up to twenty-five dollars for his work at a large funeral. In a small church this office, if it exists, is voluntary, but the sexton usually is sent a fee, which he may contribute to the church if he wishes. The organist receives a similar amount.

ℐ      ℐ      ℐ

**We had a death in our family some nine months ago. With Christmas approaching I feel I would like to send Christmas**

cards to my friends, but my mother feels that it would be disrespectful to our father. Also, my mother wants to know if you think it is all right for her to send some cards. R.C., Oak Park, Michigan

The modern feeling is that we do not shut off warm contacts with our friends during our period of mourning. Now, after three months of social restriction, most people gradually resume a normal way of living. I agree with you that you may send Christmas cards to your own friends, but they should be very conservative ones. Insofar as your mother is concerned, it depends on how she really feels about it, but there again she may now send conservative Christmas cards, or, if she prefers, little notes of Christmas greeting to her close friends.

✐ ✐ ✐

I am divorced. My former husband's death seems rather imminent. If he dies, should I accompany my children to his funeral? My children are between the ages of ten and fifteen. There has been considerable bad feeling as a result of the divorce, and perhaps my presence at the funeral would be open to criticism on the grounds of insincerity, to say the least. R.J., Birmingham, Michigan

I feel you should go, because in religious teaching death should erase such animosities. If you find that you must attend the funeral, do so for your children's sake. Keep in your mind the happiness that you must have had at some time with your former husband.

# YOUR MANNERS
# AWAY FROM HOME

## Dear Miss Vanderbilt:

### DRESS AND CUSTOMS ON SHIPS, PLANES, AND TRAINS

I am going to Europe by ship in the early spring. What sort of clothes should I take for wear aboard? What sort of things should my husband take? M.T.S., Rochester, New York

Clothing aboard ship is casual during the daytime—the sort of clothes worn at a country club in any good resort. At best they are conservative, with shorts and bathing apparel confined to the swimming and sports area. Slacks on women to whom they are becoming are seen on all decks, to some extent in the dining room for breakfast and, to a lesser extent, at lunch. Men wear coats at all meals, too, on first-class liners. They do not wear sports clothes at night in the public rooms or dining room. Women may or may not wear sports hats or scarves, as they please, on deck or at daytime meals. In the evening, except in tourist and cabin class, there is some attempt at formality, depending, of course, on the ship on which one travels. On the great transatlantic liners dinner jackets are the general, though not obligatory, rule. It is never bad taste to appear in dinner dress, and on ships where a Captain's or Gala Dinner is given, formality is expected, with men wearing dinner jackets and women appearing, if they wish, in full evening dress. On some ships this special night is made into a fancy dress affair, which permits considerable leeway in costumes. These are usually available from the ship's stores, but if you know a costume affair to be the ship's custom you may take along your own costume.

Those that win the prizes, however, are usually the ones that are extemporized out of whatever happens to be on hand in one's baggage. But quite a few diehards attend such evenings in their usual clothes and enjoy themselves nonetheless, with perhaps a paper hat added to give the right festive note.

ˀ    ˀ    ˀ

**My husband and I are taking a cruise. Are there any nights that we don't dress? We are taking dinner clothes for the really festive nights we know are planned. E.H., Salt Lake City, Utah**

On the first night and the last night aboard people don't dress for dinner but wear their ordinary travel clothes. This is because on the first night one is just unpacking and on the last night one has just packed up. The nights following shore excursions are "don't dress" nights.

ˀ    ˀ    ˀ

**Our whole family is going to Europe for the summer. Should we let our friends know that we'd like them to see us off? If so, are there any special arrangements that need to be made with the steamship company? If they ask us if we would like gifts, what do you think is suitable? Our family consists of two almost grown-up teen-age children, a boy and a girl, my husband, and myself. C.D.G., Larchmont, New York**

International traveling is becoming so very common for Americans that there is much less elaborate "seeing off" of people on boats than there used to be. However, you may certainly tell your friends the date and time of your embarkation and invite them to come aboard if they would like to. It is advisable to ask the steamship line what the permissible visiting hours are. Then, if you expect friends, get aboard with your family in plenty of time to receive the earliest comers. If friends actually ask you what you would like as a bon voyage gift, try to suggest something that you would have included in your regular luggage. The meals aboard the great liners are so varied and sumptuous these days that the old-time huge baskets of fruit given to departing voyagers often go to waste. Too many flowers, too, crowd a stateroom, and few women these days wear corsages aboard ship or elsewhere. The best gifts for the ship's passengers are books, magazines, nylons, gloves, hand-kerchiefs, cosmetics, scarves, cigarettes, underwear, compact kits of various kinds. One of the very nicest is for the visitor to make ar-rangements with the steamship company to serve a bottle of wine or champagne during the voyage with the compliments of the donor.

✓ ✓ ✓

**I have some friends who are going to Europe by air. As their closest friends, should my husband and I give them a going-away present? Are we expected to see them off? Mrs. N.G.B., Chappaqua, New York**

It is much more convenient to see friends off on such a trip by plane in your own home town rather than at the airport. There, visitors are rarely allowed beyond the gates, and farewells are very brief. As for gifts, you know that there are severe weight restrictions on luggage. Take nothing to your friends, if you do go to their point of embarkation, that will add to the weight of their luggage. If well in advance of their packing you want to give them articles of clothing in nylon and the other miracle fibers, these are always welcome to the plane traveler. Nylon stockings, tiny packets of detergents put up for travelers, airplane luggage, paperback books, plastic-packaged toiletries should all be welcome.

✓ ✓ ✓

**Under what circumstances is it all right for a man to talk to a woman when traveling? I am a friendly person and I know there are rules about this, so perhaps I am being overcautious. J.G.R., Far Rockaway, New York**

On short train and bus rides there is rarely any conversation be-tween seatmates. People read their papers and books and do not encourage conversation from strangers under these circumstances. On long bus rides and long train rides, some conversation is usual but should be kept on a highly impersonal level and names are not usually exchanged. Airplane travel is so very usual these days that sometimes one can travel halfway across the continent without say-ing a word to a seatmate. On the other hand, limited conversa-tion may be welcome. On boats one speaks to fellow passengers and enters into conversation that seems welcome without special introduction. A passenger who does not wish to engage in conversation can always answer in a monosyllable and take up reading matter which he providentially has brought with him.

✔    ✔    ✔

**When you are traveling by Pullman in an upper or lower berth, is it proper to tell a porter when you want to retire? And where do you go while he is making up the berth? L.A., Norwalk, Connecticut**

Yes, you may tell the porter at what time you would like to retire. As he has many other berths to make up, however, give him plenty of advance notice. While he is making up your berth you may sit in other unoccupied seats or go to the lounge or observation car or to the dining car. If a mother and small child occupy a whole section, it is perfectly proper to have the lower berth made up at any time during the day, if you prefer to recline during the trip. Elderly or ill people may also do the same thing, if they are occupying a section—that is, have reserved both upper and lower berths. The upper berth would not be made up, of course.

✔    ✔    ✔

**In passing a woman in a narrow corridor of a train, what should I do so that she may pass without coming into close contact with me? D.J., Mamaroneck, New York**

You step into an empty compartment if there is one, if there isn't, you flatten yourself, face inward, against either wall.

### Tipping on Ships, Planes, and Trains

**I am about to go abroad for the first time. Can you give me the rules for tipping aboard ship? G.M., New Orleans, Louisiana**

Just before debarking, a passenger tips the following personnel: room steward, table steward, headwaiter, wine steward, if he's been used, the deck and bath stewards. The steward who has taken care of your cabin receives seven-fifty to ten dollars per person as does the table steward and headwaiter. Ladies are attended by both steward and stewardess. The tip of seven-fifty to ten dollars is divided between them at the end of the voyage. Deck stewards receive one dollar or more depending on the amount of service they have rendered. Passengers without private bath tip the bath steward one dollar at the end of the voyage, and the "boots" receives one dollar for keeping shoes shined. Cabin boys are usually tipped at the time they perform their small services, if at all. Bar attendants are usually tipped at the time of service if the bill is settled at the time. If the check is signed by a regular frequenter of the smoking room, he might prefer to tip at the end of the voyage. On some ships the card-signing custom prevails, on others payment is required at the time of ordering. On most ships the chief steward is classed as a ship's officer and, as such, is never tipped.

✓    ✓    ✓

**How do you tip a Pullman porter for a short ride, and for an overnight one? R.N., Detroit, Michigan**

For a very short train ride in a Pullman, say two and one half hours, it is usual to tip the porter twenty-five cents—even if he has performed no service for you such as brushing your clothes or handling your luggage. Overnight it is usually a minimum of fifty cents per night and as much as a dollar if there has been much baggage that he has had to handle in making up your berth and in getting you off the train.

✓    ✓    ✓

**I never know how to tip aboard a train when I am having a meal and whom to tip. For example, does the head steward who comes out and seats me expect a tip or just the steward who waits on me? What about the steward in the observation car who serves drinks? D.L.C., New Brunswick, New Jersey**

A dining car steward is tipped 15 per cent of the bill, never less than a quarter per person if a meal has been served. An observation car steward who has served drinks is tipped 15 per cent of the total bar bill, not less than a quarter. The head steward is not tipped unless he has performed some very special service.

✓    ✓    ✓

**I am making my first airplane trip in a number of years. I can't remember whom you tip and what about meals on the plane? J.H.H., Paterson, New Jersey**

You do not tip anyone aboard an airplane, as all the crew have a professional status. When you pick up your luggage at the destination the airline provides porter service from the plane into the checkout area. These are staff porters and are not tipped but porters (sky caps) who take over from them and carry your luggage to waiting limousines or taxis are tipped approximately twenty-five cents per bag. On some planes now (particularly on the tourist flights) no real meals are served, but coffee and other beverages and frequently little snacks are served free. On checking in, you should inquire whether your flight serves a meal. This is part of the cost of the transportation.

*✓ ✓ ✓*

**I have not traveled frequently for many years, and I understand the regulations regarding the tipping of redcaps in railroad stations have changed and that they are often different in different localities. Can you set me right? Mrs. M.T.D., El Paso, Texas**

In most terminals redcaps get a standard price per bag, as much as thirty-five cents per bag in city areas. A tip on top of this fee is usual where the service has been prompt, courteous, and efficient. In areas where redcaps do not receive a set fee, a minimum of ten cents per bag is expected plus a tip of a quarter or more, depending on the amount and weight of the bags. In some of the big terminals self-service porterage is available. The patron pays a quarter for the cart and conveys his own luggage.

## HOTELS

**In an older etiquette book it says that when you make a reservation in a hotel by letter you should sign yourself "Mrs. John Smith," not Dorothy Smith with Mrs. John Smith beneath it, as we were taught in school. Which is correct? B.C.E., York, Pennsylvania**

I vastly prefer the second method. All business letters are written this way, and I see no reason why the manager of a hotel should be treated differently than, say, the complaint department of a department store. This use is excusable only in a telegram as it saves wordage and prevents errors.

⁊　　　⁊　　　⁊

**Can you tell me how to send a wire reserving a hotel room?** Mrs. G.K.L., Nashville, Tennessee

You send a straight wire (fifteen words permitted at the base rate) or a day or night letter if you have more time. You address it: MANAGER, GRAND HOTEL, BOSTON, MASS. PLEASE RESERVE OUTSIDE DOUBLE ROOM TWIN BEDS BATH TWO DAYS SELF AND DAUGHTER TUESDAY JUNE 8TH. ARRIVING 5 P.M. PLEASE CONFIRM. SIGNED MRS. ROGER DARWIN, 28 BRICK DRIVE, NASHVILLE, TENN. Note that this is the exception—in a telegram of this nature—in which a woman signs her name, preceding it with "Mrs." The important thing to remember is that you should mention the length of your stay, exact accommodations you want, whether or not you will be accompanied by someone else, and whether this person is to occupy your quarters or separate ones.

⁊　　　⁊　　　⁊

**I am puzzled by the travel brochures which say in the hotel ads "European plan" or "American plan." Can you explain the difference to me?** G.P., Maysville, Kentucky

European plan means room alone without meals. American plan means room and meals.

⁊　　　⁊　　　⁊

**My husband and I are going to go to Washington and take our two children, aged seven and four. How do we register at the hotel?** Mrs. J.S., Williamsburg, Virginia

You register as Mr. and Mrs. John Smith and children, New York (the full address is given if the card so indicates). If the children were older, if they were likely to receive callers or telephone calls, it would be necessary to list their names, Paul Smith and Stephen

Smith (no "Master"), and of course you may also do it in this instance, if you wish, but it is not required. A baby is listed as "Baby." A little girl, when her name is given, is listed as Miss Constance Smith. Should you be taking a servant, you list her as Miss Clara Jones, maid. It used to be that a maid was listed merely as "maid" and a chauffeur merely as "chauffeur." Today, however, most people give their employees a proper identity even under these circumstances.

*      *      *

**What is the proper procedure in checking out of a hotel?** T.K., El Paso, Texas

If you have luggage with which you need assistance, you pick up the phone and say "I'm checking out. Will you send a bellboy." If you have, say, only one small bag you wish to carry yourself, you may carry it to the lobby where you may, if you wish, refuse the services of a bellboy while checking out at the desk.

## Tipping in Hotels

**Are you supposed to tip the chambermaid in a hotel, even if you don't see her?** M.S.T., Quincy, Massachusetts

In hotels where one is a transient the tip for the chambermaid is twenty-five cents to fifty cents for an overnight stay, depending on the quality of the hotel. The tip is best left under a pillow on the bed if one leaves before the beds are made up; otherwise it may be given to the housekeeper who will see that she receives it or may be left in a marked envelope at the desk. In a hotel where one is a resident the chambermaid receives a dollar a month per room. Where a guest stays a week or two the chambermaid receives a dollar per week for each bedroom in her charge.

*      *      *

**How do you tip a hotel porter?** Mrs. H.D., Miami, Florida

A hotel porter receives twenty-five cents per trunk carried up to a room. If there is other heavy baggage as well, fifty cents. If he performs special services, such as making reservations or securing theater tickets, he receives anything from fifty cents to two or three dollars, depending on the difficulty involved.

✓    ✓    ✓

**What's the difference in tips for a bellhop who brings up your bags and for one who just delivers a telegram or brings up your mail? S.T., El Paso, Texas**

The standard tip for a bellhop carrying up luggage for a newly registered guest or couple is a quarter if he is able to bring all the luggage in one trip. If two or more trips are needed the tip advances on the basis of twenty-five cents for each trip involved. Bellhops who deliver telegrams, a newspaper, or other small things to the room receive a quarter. A large bulky package or an armful of clothes from the valet should bring him a quarter tip.

✓    ✓    ✓

**How much do page boys in hotels get for summoning guests? C.A.P., Washington, District of Columbia**

Page boys usually receive a tip of a quarter from the person paged.

✓    ✓    ✓

**I noticed a lot of hotels have servidors so that the valet can pick up your clothes and leave them for you, but you never see him. What happens if a valet brings pressed clothes back to you—to the door? Do you tip him? C.T., Charlotte, North Carolina**

Hotel valets, usually operating their own shops within a hotel, do not expect tips, except for rush jobs or those done outside of the usual hours.

✓    ✓    ✓

**I live in a residence hotel and wonder whether I am supposed to tip the elevator starter after I have been here for a few months. J.A.M.C., Miami, Florida**

A resident in a hotel usually tips elevator men regularly, giving him a dollar a month, approximately, and remembers the starter, too, at regular intervals.

✓    ✓    ✓

I live in a hotel and frequently have my meals sent up. I get confused when I order something like a pot of tea, because 10 or 15 per cent of that order would be very little for the waiter's time. Can you help me out? N.L., Toledo, Ohio

Room waiters are tipped not less than a quarter—for an individual small order such as a pot of tea and toast. For a dinner order it is 15 per cent of the bill. If wine has been served there should be an extra tip for the handling and serving of it. Guests may add a notation at the bottom of the bill concerning the amount of the tip they wish given the room waiter. Resident guests tip room waiters for each service, too, but usually see that head room waiters receive a tip about twice a year, the tip depending on the amount of room service the guest requires—a minimum of five dollars each time and possibly as much as ten.

✓    ✓    ✓

It certainly seems to me that a disproportionate amount of my income goes for tipping, as I travel a lot in my work. For instance, should I tip a hotel doorman just for opening the door of my cab? J.A., Jamaica, New York

No, not if he performs no other service. If, however, he helps to unload the cab with a great deal of your luggage, even though he just takes it to the entrance of the hotel, he expects a tip—perhaps a quarter. If he must go out in the rain to find you a cab in the midst of traffic, you gauge the tip by the amount of trouble he has had. You might give him twenty-five cents, or even fifty cents, or on a stormy night or very late, as much as a dollar if he has a hard time finding a cab. Those who seek shelter under a hotel marquee in the rain (especially if they are not guests at the hotel) tip the doorman anything from a quarter to a dollar for summoning a cab, depending on the difficulty he has had in procuring one.

## RESTAURANTS

Who goes first into a restaurant, a lady or her escort? J.H., St. Louis, Missouri

On entering a restaurant door a lady goes first if there is an attendant to hold the door open for her, otherwise her escort provides this service. Once inside, the man moves his companion out of the traffic, checks his things, then moves at her side, or slightly in advance, to the entrance to the dining room. There, if the captain comes to meet them, the lady steps forward and follows him to the table indicated, allowing herself to be seated. If there is no captain, her escort leads the way into the dining room, locates a table, and seats his companion himself. On leaving, the man goes first, making a pathway for the lady. If the captain comes forward to see them out, the man then steps back and lets the lady follow the captain. But an escorted lady is never left to make her way through a crowded restaurant alone.

↑    ↑    ↑

**Another couple often goes with us to restaurants. They are about our age and I wonder what is the proper way for the women to be seated. What happens when we are dining with a couple that is very much older? L.N., Quincy, Massachusetts**

When two young couples seat themselves at a table, the women take chairs opposite each other. If one man is the host, he tries to seat himself so the woman to be honored is at his right even if it is his wife—for example, on her birthday or their anniversary. No great point, however, need be made these days over the seating at a banquette (built-in wall seats). If a younger couple is dining with a much older one, the older couple is offered the wall seats and the younger couple sits together on the aisle so that the younger man is opposite the older woman. When two women are seated together opposite the two men, they sit opposite their own escorts—husband or not.

↑    ↑    ↑

**When dining in a restaurant, does the hostess give the entire order for the guests or are individual orders taken by the waiter or waitress? When just two—man and woman—dine together, who gives the order? Mrs. D.A.N., Evanston, Illinois**

When a number of people sit down together in a restaurant, it is much simpler if individual orders are taken by the waiter or waitress, unless the host or hostess has ordered the entire dinner, the same for everyone, in advance. When just two, a man and a woman, dine together, the man asks the woman what she would like to have—perhaps makes some suggestions—and gives the order to the waiter. If the dinner is table d'hôte the waiter asks the woman what she will have and takes the order from her.

At an intimate restaurant dinner where the host or hostess's voice can clearly be heard the length of the table, a guest may accept the card from the waiter and make a selection, but he then waits for his host to ask him what he would like and permits his host to place the order. At a table of women where there is no question of there being a hostess but all plan to pay for themselves, orders are always given individually, even in a very small group such as four.

*   *   *

**When two couples or more have dinner out, is the bill afterward to be split evenly or is each couple to pay for what they ordered? For instance, if one couple orders hamburgers and the other sirloin steak, one couple does not order drinks and the other does, when the check comes do even the drinks have to be paid for by the non-drinker? This has caused hard feelings. My husband feels that if he orders less he should not be expected to pay a split bill at the end of the evening. E.R., Oakland, California**

If there is a large discrepancy between the amounts spent by the two couples, it is perfectly acceptable for the man of the couple which spent less to say, "Let me figure out what we owe on this." Where there is very little difference it might be considered niggardly to be meticulous about the division of cost.

*   *   *

**In a night club, when a large party enters with the host and hostess, shouldn't the maître d' seat the guests to avoid confusion? T.E.R., Yuma, Arizona**

No. The maître d' does not know the guests and wouldn't know where to place them so that all will be congenial. The hostess seats her guests, or, if there is a host alone, he performs this function.

*   *   *

We like to dine at a smörgåsbord restaurant. When we take guests should I, as hostess, lead them to the table, or should I let the men, including my husband, go to the table and choose the women's food? Or doesn't it matter who goes first to the table? Mrs. L.E.J., Adrian, Michigan

A smörgåsbord meal is very informal, but you could lead the way to the table. If the restaurant is very crowded and there is no waiter to clear the way for you, your husband would go first, followed by any of your women guests. He could offer to serve his companion or merely hand her a plate and suggest that she make her own selections. People usually prefer to do this at the bounteous board.

*     *     *

Recently, when four of us were dining out—two married couples—one of the husbands left the table for a few minutes. The remaining husband, left with his wife and the wife of the other, lit the cigarette first of his friend's wife, then of his own. His wife felt that as her escort he should have lit her cigarette first. Which is correct? Mrs. R.L.V., Columbus, Ohio

As one woman was left alone, the husband and wife remaining are, in effect, her host and hostess for the moment. Therefore it was correct for the remaining husband to light the guest's cigarette first, then his wife's.

*     *     *

Recently I was a guest at a club luncheon in a restaurant. Accidentally, I overturned my tomato juice. What was the right thing to do? The waiter didn't see the accident immediately. Mrs. R.B.C., South Bend, Indiana

A waiter seeing such an accident would immediately change the cloth, or, if that was impossible at a long table, would spread a clean napkin or small cloth over the spilled food. As the waiter did not do this because he was busy elsewhere at such a large luncheon, you could have spread a napkin over the spot yourself, without undue discussion of the incident. Everyone occasionally has things like this happen.

*     *     *

Three or four of us men executives meet once or twice a week for lunch in a near-by restaurant. Our practice is for the first one there to reserve a table. But if one is late, must the others wait before seating themselves and beginning the meal? J.A.L., New York, New York

The first one to arrive tells the headwaiter or hostess how many he is expecting in his party. When the majority have arrived, they seat themselves, leaving word that they have gone on in. For a whole party to wait for the late-comer may mean that they cannot get a table reservation at all. For them to seat themselves and then try to wait until the missing guest arrives would be to hold up the restaurant unfairly. If the late-comer is a client or superior, however, the others do wait outside, even though this may mean a delay in getting a table when they want it. When there is a long line, the headwaiter or hostess usually assigns a number to a party. If the party is late assembling, you merely say that you do not want the table at the time that it is offered but will let the hostess or headwaiter know when your party is all together.

✓  ✓  ✓

What do you do with the wrapper on a lump of sugar when you are dining out in a restaurant? Do you put it on the tablecloth, in the saucer of your cup, or in the ash tray? E.F., Toledo, Ohio

This is one of those things for which there is no real rule. You just use common sense. I would say put it on the tablecloth, for if you put it in the ash tray it may start a fire, and if you put it in your saucer it may cause the cup to tip over when you put it back in the saucer after taking a drink. If it is on the tablecloth the waiter will clear it off along with crumbs.

✓  ✓  ✓

My friend always insists on wiping off the table silver with his napkin when we go out to restaurants, cheap or expensive. I claim it is just a bad habit with him. He insists it is a sanitary precaution. Should he do this? N.J., Pasadena, California

He should not do this, even in cheap restaurants. If the silver seems dirty he should quickly ask the waiter to replace it with clean silver.

If there is any reluctance on the part of the waiter or of the manager, a complaint should be sent to the Department of Health. No one who must or who chooses to eat in a restaurant in this country need be exposed to any unsanitary conditions. He need only insist on his rights. From a practical standpoint, of course, a dry napkin, however clean, is not going to remove any dirt from the utensils. Soap and hot water are called for.

✓ ✓ ✓

**Will you please tell me what you consider the correct way of disposing of the small tea bag on a string served in a cup of tea in most restaurants these days. It seems kind of messy to remove it and place it in the saucer beside the cup, but, with no special dish provided to hold it, just what should be done with it? Mrs. T.L.B., Salem, Massachusetts**

The only thing to do is to lift it by the tag and perhaps let it drain a little before placing it in the saucer. If you have a butter plate and wish to place it there, that is also permissible. The very best solution of course, for the restaurant, would be to serve the tea in individual pots so that the tea bags could stay out of sight.

✓ ✓ ✓

**What's the proper way to get the attention of a waiter or waitress in a restaurant? P.K., Meriden, Connecticut**

A good waiter or waitress is attentive at all times to the possible needs of the patron. All that should be necessary in a properly staffed restaurant is for the diner to lift his hand—or one finger—in a summoning gesture. If this fails to get attention, the diner calls softly, "Waiter!," or "Waitress!," (not "Miss!"). Glass rapping, a European expedient, should be resorted to only in desperation. You may also ask another waiter or waitress to fetch yours.

✓ ✓ ✓

**When there is no host or hostess—for example, when friends are eating together in a restaurant—when does one pick up his napkin, and is it still good manners to hold one's left hand in the lap? Mr. R.J.L., Denver, Colorado**

When there is no host or hostess, the diner picks up his napkin as soon as he is seated, but if there are ladies present they take the initiative. When you leave the table temporarily, put the napkin casually to the left of the place setting. A dinner napkin should not be shaken out or tucked in (except for children), but it is laid lengthwise across the knees. It should be used to dab the lips whenever necessary—especially before one drinks any beverage. Such drinks, by the way, should be taken only when the mouth is empty.

It is optional whether the left hand, when one is eating, is held in the lap, American style, or resting in a relaxed fashion to the left of the place setting, European style. I prefer the latter as more natural, because it gives better balance to the body. But there should be no lounging at the table.

✓   ✓   ✓

**A date and I went to a neighborhood restaurant to eat dinner Sunday night. The only available seats were in a booth for four in which a lone man was already seated. I asked my date to ask this man to share the booth with us. My date said that was not correct and refused to do so. Was he right? A.L.C., Dallas, Texas**

It depends on the policy of the restaurant. In a self-service restaurant you take any available seat. In a restaurant with service, especially in one with a headwaiter or hostess, you wait to be assigned to seats. Most restaurants try to seat lone diners at tables for two or one, but where this is impossible they usually do not ask that such accommodations as a booth be shared with strangers. Under crowded conditions, restaurants sometimes ask a man to share a table with another man but not with a woman and vice versa. I feel that your date was right and that essentially his objection was to having your privacy disturbed by a stranger. How could conversation be possible under such circumstances? You might have had an embarassing situation had the stranger decided to join your conversation. This is the sort of thing that good restaurants try to avoid.

### Tipping in Restaurants

**I am not always certain who to tip and how much to tip in restaurants. Can you help me? P.W., Woonsocket, Rhode Island**

If one frequents a certain restaurant, it is not necessary for him to tip the headwaiter on each occasion, unless he has had special consideration—worked out the menu in advance with the headwaiter, had his table changed, or ordered some spectacular dish such as crêpes suzette, the completion of which has been presided over by this factotum. The tip is given on the way out. When the headwaiter is also an owner of the place he receives no tip but is thanked on the way out if he shows out his guests.

Such a tip is quietly slipped into the waiting palm in an unobvious manner, but if the room headwaiter is not at his post he is not sought out by the patron. The tendered tip in an expensive place is usually two to five dollars. In a less elaborate establishment it is certainly never silver—always at least a dollar.

The wine steward, if his services have been enlisted, receives 10 per cent of the bill in round figures. Where drinks begun at the bar have been brought with the bar bill to the table later, the bartender receives his 10 per cent.

In restaurants that employ headwaiters for sections—men who do no more than take the order and pass it on to table waiters for execution—no tip is expected by the section headwaiter, unless, of course, special service has been requested in which he has taken some active part. In that case his tip is not less than a dollar bill and may be two dollars if the party comprises more than two people.

A waiter receives 15 per cent to 20 per cent (depending on the place) in round figures (don't leave pennies on the plate unless they add up to an even amount). If the bill has been very small, then he should receive a minimum of ten cents per person; in night clubs, twenty-five cents per person, minimum.

A cigarette girl usually arranges her change to indicate what she'd like to get, but ten or fifteen cents surcharge on a pack of cigarettes is enough and no one need feel like Shylock for picking up the additional change from a dollar bill.

The bus boy is not tipped. In a nightclub or expensive restaurant the attendants in the men's and women's lounges usually put decoy coins on a plate to indicate what they expect in the way of a tip, as does the hatcheck girl. Unless some service has been asked, the tip need not be, for instance, a quarter, but can well be ten cents.

Doormen who perform a service—secure a taxi, summon or

bring your parked car—usually receive a quarter. At an inexpensive place, if just a taxi has been summoned in good weather
and the job has entailed no more than his blowing his whistle, a
dime is sufficient.

✶    ✶    ✶

**Why aren't bus boys in hotels and restaurants tipped?** J.L., Houston,
Texas

Because the waiter for whom he clears the tables shares his tips
with him. In resort hotels, however, student bus boys *are* tipped.

✶    ✶    ✶

**In a restaurant, is it okay to leave an extra large tip for especially
good service and vice versa for very poor service? Or should one
leave the usual standard tip regardless of the quality of the service,
whether it is very poor or extremely good?** C.S., Montclair, New
Jersey

Anyone who works at a job should have pride in what he does
and the way he does it. Most waiters and waitresses do an excellent job and try to please their customers. Occasionally, however,
one gets surly and inefficient service. I believe in reward and punish-
ment. If you believe the service has been deliberately bad—in
effect, no service at all—and if you have the courage to do so,
leave no tip. If the service is good, always commend either with
a kind word or with a little extra on the tip if you can afford it.
While we should think of a tip as additional payment for service,
certainly it is not required where the services were nil.

✶    ✶    ✶

**When I was in Chicago I saw one restaurant there that had the
checkroom attendant on its payroll, and it had a row of boxes
labeled with the names of various charities. There was a sign explaining that tipping was not permitted, but that patrons could if
they wished donate to these various charities. I thought this was a
very nice idea. However, in most restaurants you are expected to
tip. What's the rule?** L.A., South Norwalk, Connecticut

I, too, think that Chicago restaurant had a very good idea. I know
it's very hard sometimes for a man to have to retrieve his hat at the

price of the expected tip. If he moves around much this can be very expensive. However, here is the rule. At any checkroom in a hotel specially set up to serve a special affair such as a dance or ball, the attendant receives a quarter per person. At a mere cloak-room outside a hotel restaurant the usual tip is ten cents, despite the quarter "decoys" on the plate.

❦  ❦  ❦

**My husband and I are going to a big testimonial dinner at a hotel. We've bought our own tickets but will be at a table with others we don't know. What does my husband do about tips—if anything?** Mrs. J.D.B., Toledo, Ohio

At public dinners there is sometimes a small card on each table which reads, "Gratuities have been taken care of by the Dinner Committee"—a very good idea. If there is no such card at the table, the waiters, immediately after the service of dessert and coffee and before the speaking begins, come to the host or hostess of each table and place a silver salver before him or her, often with a murmured explanation that something is expected for the table's waiters. Unless all at the table are personally invited guests, the host or hostess makes no attempt to tip for the whole table but after placing a dollar (per service for which he or she feels responsible) on the tray, directs the waiter to the gentlemen at the table, each of whom should leave (at an $8.00 to $10.00 per plate dinner) a dollar for himself and one for the lady he escorts. Women should never be approached for tips if there are gentlemen at the table.

## THEATERS

**What do you do with ticket stubs? Is it necessary to hold on to them until the end of the show?** Mrs. S.D., Long Island City, New York

Yes, you hold on to them even after you are seated. Someone else may dispute your right to the seats. Or, if you go out during intermission, you are sometimes required to show them before getting into the theater again. If you are entertaining at the theater for business reasons, it is important to keep the stub as a record for tax purposes.

✓  ✓  ✓

**If you are entertaining another couple at the theater, how are they seated?** R.E.N., Newark, New Jersey

The host (or hostess, in a party of women) produces the tickets at the door and stands back to let the guests file in. Guests then wait until the host or hostess precedes them with the usher to their seats. The hostess in a mixed group places a man first in a line of seats so a woman guest need not sit next to a stranger. She also places a man, usually the host, on the aisle—or in the seat nearest the aisle. When two couples are being seated, the two women sit together in such an arrangement.

## CARS AND PUBLIC CONVEYANCES

**When a couple takes a trip together in a car, should the wife of the driver sit with him or should the two women sit together in the back seat and the two men together in the front? What if a chauffeur is driving? Who sits with him? Where does the wife of the owner sit?** Mrs. S.M.G., New York, New York

In the first instance, the wife of the driver usually sits with him, but it is mainly a matter of choice and convenience. If the two men have much to discuss and would like to ride together from time to time that is all right, too. If both women wish to sit together they may. If one person finds that sitting in the back causes car sickness he should say so and may then be given a front seat. In a large car three may sit in front if that is convenient for the driver. In this case this might mean that the two women would sit in the front with the wife of the driver in the center seat. In a chauffeur-driven car the owner's seat is to the right, and guests entering a limousine courteously take seats to the left, for it is presumably from the right-hand rear seat that the owner can best direct his or her chauffeur. However, this is not a hard and fast rule, and the owner may certainly give the seat to a guest. When all seats in a car are to be used the car owner usually indicates who is to sit with the chauffeur. If there is a young man passenger in the car it is usually he who is asked to sit there. Or if a servant is traveling the servant sits in the front seat. If all the other passengers are ladies the owner himself sits with the chauffeur.

✓      ✓      ✓

**What is the correct tipping procedure for taxis in city areas? Mr. I.B., Allentown, Pennsylvania**

For taxi fares which come to fifty cents or less, you should never give a tip of less than fifteen cents. If the fare is between fifty cents and a dollar, give twenty cents. And for a fare of over a dollar, you should figure out the tip for the driver the same way you would for a waiter in a restaurant. This would mean at least 15 per cent of the total.

✓      ✓      ✓

**Should you give guests a choice of car seats if they haven't started out with you? Or should a guest you pick up just take whatever seat is still available? T.J.R., Tampa, Florida**

To change everyone around might delay departure so the guest takes the remaining seat, but this should never be a jump seat while an able member of the family or a young person occupies a more comfortable one. But never hold up traffic while you shift the seating—proceed somewhere out of traffic first.

✓      ✓      ✓

**Who gets out of a taxi first, a man or woman? H.A.N., Chicago, Illinois**

Men are so indoctrinated with the idea that a lady always goes first that they become confused about who should alight first from a vehicle. A man always goes first in this case, turns and assists the lady down from or out of the vehicle by offering her his *hand*, not his arm. In assisting her *up into* vehicles he places his hand under the crook of her elbow for support, allowing her to go first.

✓      ✓      ✓

When you call a taxi for a woman whom you are unable to accompany to her destination, how do you arrange to pay her fare? It seems awkward to offer her the money, and it isn't always possible to judge what the fare will be. How would you handle this? R.C., San Francisco, California

No, don't thrust the cab fare at the woman. Ask the driver what the approximate fare will be and pay him in advance, including the tip. If the appointment was a business rather than a social one, he has no such responsibility, and if the woman asks him to summon a cab she should pay her own fare. For a man to put a woman into a cab she has not requested with the assumption that she has enough money with her to pay for it is to place her, perhaps, in an embarrassing position.

## PUBLIC SPEAKING

Do you feel that a woman public speaker must always wear a hat? M.M., Oakland, California

Not necessarily. She doesn't wear one if she is in evening clothes. In many quite urban communities, where hatlessness is a matter of choice, I've seen many distinguished women speakers without hats. In very small communities, which tend to be conservative in this matter, it is probably well for the speaker to wear a hat in order to avoid criticism. It should not be the kind that will shade her face or distract the audience, however. Any arrangement of a veil, flowers, or perhaps a velvet ribbon bow would be quite acceptable.

## TIPPING FOR SPECIAL SERVICES

### Hairdressers and Barber Shops

I live in a small town and go to a beauty shop operated by the woman who owns it. She has one extra operator, but she herself usually takes care of me. Now the question is, do I tip her? And when I go into the nearest city, what's the usual there in beauty parlors? Do you tip all of the people who serve you in some way? This gets very expensive, if so. E.J., New Milford, Connecticut

The operator of a shop with little or no help does not usually expect a tip, because he is self-employed. The operator of a big city shop where there are many employees and who himself has customers is often tipped on the same scale as are his employees. If he is the kind of operator who has a supervisory job mainly and who takes only an occasional customer, he is usually not tipped, for he is classed as an artist of professional standing. In most beauty shops the tip varies, depending on the location of the shop and the cost of the services. In very expensive shops each operator who serves you, plus the maid who takes your coat, is tipped. The manicurist receives twenty-five to fifty cents or even more, depending on what the charges are for the manicure. If a separate operator does the shampooing she is tipped a quarter. An operator who cuts and sets your hair gets from fifty cents to a dollar or more, depending on the cost of the service she renders. The maid who takes your coat will get a minimum of a dime and as much as a quarter if she performs some special little service for you.

✓ ✓ ✓

When I take my son to the barber shop the price for his haircut is $1.25. What tip should I leave if his hair is cut by the man who owns the shop and what if it is cut by one of his employees? When my own hair is cut in a beauty shop what tip should I leave? My husband goes to a barber shop that charges him $1.50 for a haircut. What would be an appropriate tip? Mrs. T.A.K., Minneapolis, Minnesota

For a man's haircut of $1.50, a quarter tip is about right. For a man's or woman's haircut or trim, if it is $2.00 or $2.50, fifty cents is about right. If it's over that, tip about 20 per cent of the bill if you've had no other services. If the haircut is included in the other services of a beauty parlor tip as above.

## Taxis

In most cities taxi drivers are courteous to their patrons and thank them for whatever tip they may care to give them. However, on a recent trip to New York I found that no matter what I tipped a New York taxi driver he was more likely not to thank me than to thank me. It so happens that even though I am a woman I am inclined to overtip. Maybe they expect a small tip from me because I'm a woman. Do you think women do undertip generally? By the way, what is the standard taxi tip in metropolitan areas? What about country areas where metered cabs aren't used? R.N.O., San Francisco, California

In general, women are thought to undertip, but I find that women who have been in business tend to tip on the same scale as do men. It seems to me, too, that more and more New York taxi drivers are taking their tips without thanks. The patron doesn't discover this until after he's given the tip, of course, so he has no redress. A well-known columnist strikes back when this happens by getting out of the cab on the side opposite the driver and leaving the door wide open so that the driver must go around and close his door. Perhaps this little discipline works, I don't know. Taxi drivers should know, of course, that the patron is not required to leave a tip. However, the expected tip for a city driver is ten or fifteen cents for any trip under fifty cents, fifteen cents to a quarter for a ride of a dollar or a little more, and proportionate amounts for rides that go over two dollars. On unmetered cabs in country areas, quarter tips are given occasionally—but not necessarily always—by regular charge customers. They are always given when luggage is handled. For the occasional customer 10 per cent to 15 per cent of the over-all charge for the journey is usual.

## Hospitals

I expect my first baby very soon and I have made my hospital arrangements. I am going to have a private nurse part of the time and then will have floor nursing. I'll have a private room. Do I tip the nurses and, if so, how much? Mrs. P.DeB., Larchmont, New York

No, you never tip nurses, for they are professional people. You may, however, give your own nurse a gift when she leaves you— books, candy, stockings, handkerchiefs, lingerie (but only for a woman patient to give), costume jewelry, a plant, or cut flowers are all possibilities. A pleasant new custom is that of sending flowers to one's nurse, either when you leave the hospital or when her duty with you terminates. These may either be flowers for her room or home, as the case may be, or may be flowers for her to wear off duty.

### Deliveries

Is it proper to tip the carry-out boys at the large supermarkets? I know some give tips and others do not. Most of these boys are high school students. "Housewife," Bridgeport, Connecticut

Yes, tip a quarter unless the market has put this service charge on your bill.

✓    ✓    ✓

I would like to know how much to tip a boy who delivers flowers and how much to tip a boy who delivers a telegram. A.G.S., Cleveland, Ohio

This is a matter of personal choice. Some people tip in these two categories, others do not. In the case of a florist's boy the tip ranges from fifteen cents to a quarter. A boy with a telegram gets between a dime and a quarter but in neither case is a tip generally expected except in hotels. In large apartment houses deliveries are made through the superintendent and such messengers do not see the householder. The important thing to remember about tipping, if it becomes a serious financial burden (which it can), is that one does not have to tip. And certainly no one should be expected to tip beyond his means, no matter what is customary.

✓    ✓    ✓

Why don't you mention letter carriers in what you write about tipping? Our letter carriers are underpaid and receive little overtime pay during the year. All carriers look forward to their Christmas gratuities and to the "Big Pay Day" on January 2nd, when they are paid for their long hours just previous to Christmas. It is practically the only time carriers are permitted overtime pay as the department is anxious to keep down expenditures and forbids overtime the rest of the year. I can inform you that the great majority of the public who do remember the letter carrier do so with cash. And that is the way he prefers it. W.B.L., Paterson, New Jersey

It has long been assumed by many people that civil service workers have such a dignified status that a tip might offend them. However, economic pressure has evidently brought about a change here, too. The average gratuity to the letter carrier where money is given seems now to be five dollars in rural and suburban communities where deliveries are often difficult in winter. In cities where the postman is rarely seen by tenants there is less sense of personal service. However, at Christmas in some cities the carriers frequently deliver in person through the buildings and receive an average of $2.00 each, and tips are usually left in mailboxes, otherwise.

# CORRESPONDENCE

## *Dear Miss Vanderbilt:*

### STATIONERY

On a man's stationery is the name printed "Mr. John Doe" or simply "John Doe"? For instance, on the envelopes, should it ever be printed or written "Return to Mr. John Doe" or should it be "Return to John Doe"? J.A.D., Burlington, Vermont

A man's stationery is printed or engraved "John Doe," and that is how his return address reads, too.

✔   ✔   ✔

I want to have some social stationery engraved for my husband, who is a doctor. Should it read "James Thomas, M.D.," with his address, or should it read "Dr. James Thomas," or should I also just use his initials, and, if so, what should they be like and where placed? What is a good size for a man's social stationery? S.N.G., New York, New York

At the top of his stationery you may use your husband's name and title with or without the address. It should read "Doctor James Thomas." In the case of a very long name the title may be abbreviated to "Dr." If you use initials they may be dye-stamped in color or be in simple block form at the top of his stationery or upper left. Or if you prefer you may use his address alone, complete with zip code, upper center, with or without his telephone number. Size 7¼ by 10¼ is good for a man's stationery and is suitable

for both typewriter and longhand. It should be in cream or gray
or white with engraving or printing in black, blue, dark green, or
perhaps maroon.

✓     ✓     ✓

**I want to order some nice personal stationery for my husband.
What is the best color and is it correct to have his name at the top?**
D.E.P., Flint, Michigan

A man's social paper should look masculine—in size, in color, and
in quality. He sticks to cream, white, or gray with engraving or
printing in black, blue, dark green, or perhaps maroon. He may
use his initials, dye-stamped in color or in simple block form at
the top of his stationery or upper left, or his name, Geoffrey
Lansing (no Mr., of course), with or without the address. Or he
uses the address, upper center, alone, with or without his telephone number. Where return address is desired on the flap, the
engraver usually uses the same dye he used on the paper itself to
save cost. If the paper is printed, just the address alone may be
used on the flap, if you desire. If the name is also used, it is used
without "Mr."

✓     ✓     ✓

**When I was a girl I was taught that a lady never used any
stationery other than white, unless perhaps it was blue or gray.
Now I find stationery, and inks!, in all colors of the rainbow.
What do you think about this?** Mrs. W.R., Monterey, California

There are all kinds of note papers for women these days, some of
them much too fancy for my taste. For some correspondence,
however, the old rule of pale blue, gray or white should hold (see
replying to wedding invitations, page 93, letters of condolence,
page 109). For a conservative correspondence, only blue or black
ink should be used. For social correspondence where special papers
are used, they may be used with contrasting inks, now so widely
available. The use of green, brown, or violet ink is now quite acceptable for informal social correspondence. Green ink and even
brown ink are used even in business if it is co-related with the
letterhead. Red ink may be used at Christmas for addressing and

signing cards and for invitations. A rose red ink can be effective when it matches a monogram on gray or white paper at any time of the year.

## LETTER WRITING AND SIGNING YOUR NAME

**Would you help me in the matter of letter salutations? In school we were taught to use "Dear Sir" on business letters, but is this the correct form when writing to a company or business where usually a secretary handles the mail? Mrs. H.B., Bay City, Michigan**

When you are writing to someone in a firm, a man whom you don't know, his name and address is at the upper left of the page in this manner:

Mr. John Brown,
The Ajax Corporation,
47 Main Street,
Ridgefield, Conn. 06877

Dear Sir:

If you have been writing regularly to Mr. Brown, your salutation may be "Dear Mr. Brown."

When you are writing to a corporation and do not know the name of anyone to address there, the form is:

The Ajax Corporation,
47 Main Street,
Ridgefield, Conn. 06877

Gentlemen:
(Unless you know it is an all-women's organization, in which case it would be "Mesdames," or, if you prefer, "Ladies.")
The usual form of closing is, in a case like this, "Sincerely," or "Sincerely yours." It is important to put on a business letter your own return address, both on the letter itself and on the envelope. You should also be careful to include the date—not merely

"Tuesday," as you would use it in a social letter—but the month and the day and the year, so that the company may file your letter correctly.

**When you are writing to a woman in business and you don't know whether she is "Mrs." or "Miss," what do you do?** J.A., Willow Run, Michigan

You address her as "Miss." When you receive a letter signed "Anne Smith" with no "Miss" in front of it, you assume that she is "Miss." If she is "Mrs.," she properly places beneath her name in parentheses the information—"(Mrs. John Smith)" for the guidance of those wishing to write her.

**When writing a business letter, do you sign thus: "Mrs. John Jones, Richmond, Utah," or "Mary Jones" and under it in parentheses "Mrs. John Jones" and no address except the heading of your letter?** A.L.B., Richmond, Utah

In writing a business letter, the usual procedure is to write your address and the date, including the year, clearly in the upper right-hand corner. Just before the salutation you write, upper left, the name of the person you are addressing, the name of the company, and its address. If you have no name in the company to whom to direct your letter you write "Gentlemen." A married woman signs such a lettter "Mary Jones" and under her signature "(Mrs. John Jones)." An unmarried woman signs herself "Mary Green" and writes "(Miss)" in front if she wishes, although it is assumed that she is "Miss" unless she had indicated to the contrary. She may also type or print beneath her signature, especially if it is not legible (Miss Mary Green). She should use the "(Miss)" if her first name is one used by both men and women—for example, "Cecil."

**My son, fifteen, is in boarding school. When I write him, do I address him as "Master," "Mister," or as plain "Robert Brown?"** J.A.B., New York, New York

As plain "Robert Brown." He is "Master" until the age of twelve, and today "Mister" beginning at age eighteen. Previously, socially, a man did not use the title, "Mister," before the age of twenty-one, but with draft age eighteen, it is now accepted that a boy reaches manhood at that age and is certainly entitled to a "Mister."

✓ ✓ ✓

**When sending a card or letter to a doctor (male or female) how is the envelope addressed?** Mrs. M.L.K., Pittsburgh, Pennsylvania

If you are paying a bill you may address him either as "Dr. George Johnson" or as "George Johnson, M.D." If you are writing to him socially you must address him as "Dr. George Johnson." Your check for medical services should read George Johnson, M.D. This is a tax precaution as Dr. George Johnson isn't necessarily an M.D.

✓ ✓ ✓

**I am writing to a friend in England whose friends use "Esquire" after his name in writing. Should I do the same when sending a formal engraved card to him?** D.C.B., Buffalo, New York

Yes, for all formal purposes. For ordinary letters "Esq." is quite correct. "Esquire" was originally used as a lesser English title. It indicated a knight's eldest son and the younger male members of a noble house whose hereditary title was borne only by the oldest male heir. Now professional men and all those working in the so-called genteel callings—arts, letters, music—and members of the House of Commons and the landed gentry are addressed in writing with "Esq." following their names. Often, too, older gentlemen of standing are called "Squire" in conversation. It might be interesting to note here that should one be sending engraved invitations to England they are always addressed to the wife alone. Where there is no inner envelope one writes on the top of the invitation "Mr. and Mrs. Brown." If there is an inner envelope, as in a wedding invitation, the phrase "Mr. and Mrs. Brown" appears on the inner envelope alone. Greeting cards, however, are addressed "Mr. and Mrs. Brown" when sent to England and the various Crown colonies where this same social procedure is followed.

✓   ✓   ✓

**What is the proper form of address for a married woman, for a widow, for a divorcée?** A.F.L., New Haven, Connecticut

A married woman is always "Mrs. John Smith," not "Mrs. Ann Smith." A widow is always "Mrs. John Smith," no matter how long she remains a widow (and incidentally she does not transfer her wedding ring to the right hand, although she may choose not to wear it). A divorcée usually takes her maiden name, "Jones," and adds it to her former married name, becoming "Mrs. Jones Smith," which identifies her much better than if she were "Mrs. Ann Smith."

✓   ✓   ✓

**You have said, I know, you prefer the use of the maiden name of a married woman as a middle name for the sake of clarity; that is, "Jane Doe Smith." What happens when "Jane Doe Smith" becomes a widow and in a few years remarries, this time to "John Adams?" Would her name then be "Jane Doe Adams" or "Jane Smith Adams?" I am asking this question from a legal standpoint, realizing that socially she could use either form.** M.S.W., Pittsburgh, Pennsylvania

Actually there is no choice here. Once she is married to another man, she ceases to use, legally and socially, the name of her former husband. Therefore, she is correctly "Jane Doe Adams," which indicates that she was born "Doe." Socially she is "Mrs. John Adams." Legally she signs herself "Jane Marie Adams," "Jane Doe Adams," "Jane Adams," or even sometimes "Mrs. John Adams," depending either on the name, if any, used in the paper she is signing or on some indicated legal requirement.

✓   ✓   ✓

**Is it ever correct for a married woman to sign her name "Sincerely, Mrs. R. C. Jones?"** S.C.L., Long Island City, New York

I cannot say often enough that a woman always signs herself with her given name plus her maiden name or married name. If she is also "Mrs. Robert Jones," she writes this in parentheses beneath her signature, if the person to whom she is writing doesn't know this. A single woman may put "Miss" in parentheses before her name to anyone who doesn't know that she is "Miss," and especially if her name is also one used by both men and women, for example, "Marion."

✓ ✓ ✓

**I am separated from my husband. When writing my name should I use my husband's full name or should I use my first name, then, of course, his last name? I.S., Fort Wayne, Indiana**

Although separated you are still married to your husband. Therefore you are "Mrs. John Smith." Should you get a divorce you would become "Mrs. Worth Smith" (combining your maiden name with your married name). If you should divorce you should not, except in business (if this seems unavoidable), become "Mrs. Mary Smith."

✓ ✓ ✓

**My father-in-law died recently. My husband is a "Junior." My mother-in-law is still alive. Does my husband drop the "Junior" and because of this give me my mother-in-law's name, or should he retain the "Junior" until she dies? D.E.B., Albany, New York**

Your husband drops the "Junior." Your mother-in-law continues to use her husband's name unless and until she remarries. But if she lives near you and there is any possibility of confusion, she may add to it "Sr." After the death of his father a man keeps "Jr." only if he was the son of a very prominent man whose name continues in the news long after his death and who therefore might be confused with his son.

✓ ✓ ✓

**I am a successful businesswoman with my own business. For many years my husband and I ran it together, and I used his name. Last year I became a widow, and now I am getting married again. Everybody knows me in business under my former husband's name. Should I try to change my name in business to my new social one? H.E.W., Elizabeth, New Jersey**

This a question which many married businesswomen have had to solve by keeping the name of a former husband because in business it has become somewhat of a trademark. It is an awkward decision to make, but the alternative, if you are very well established and have been so for many years, is to re-educate all of your business acquaintances throughout the country to call you by a new name, something which may be difficult to accomplish. Your dilemma points up the wisdom of Lucy Stoneism to a certain degree. It has always seemed wise to me for a woman who establishes herself in business or a profession to use her maiden name. I believe this gives protection, too, to her husband, should she engage in any activities that might run counter to his own professional or business interests.

✓ ✓ ✓

**With a joint checking account, is it correct for the wife to sign checks "Mrs. John Jones?"** K.A.R., Richmond, Utah

The correct way to sign checks drawn on a joint account depends on what is on the signature card at the bank. This usually reads "John and/or Mary Jones." The wife may use a middle name or initial for more complete identification if her first name and her husband's name are common.

✓ ✓ ✓

**After discovering the convenience of the typewriter, I began typing all my personal letters. This makes them easier to read because my handwriting is poor, and proper punctuation is often left out of handwritten correspondence. While typewritten letters do not have the "personal touch," I believe they benefit the receiver in that there is no time lost in deciphering illegible words. However, some of my friends object to typewritten letters. Would you be kind enough to give me your opinion on the subject?** B.J.G., Linden, New Jersey

This strikes a note of sympathy with me, as my own handwriting is highly illegible, and I know that many of my friends would prefer not to hear from me, rather than get a letter in longhand which leaves them baffled. The use of the typewriter in social correspondence is completely acceptable now, with three exceptions—letters of condolence, the bride's thank-you letters, and letters of felicitation in the case of a wedding or an engagement should be handwritten. But otherwise social letters may be typewritten, may even be dictated on social stationery.

✓   ✓   ✓

**Please settle an argument between my husband and myself. I say he can write his name "the Second," since his father's brother had the same name. He says he can't. Who is right? W.B.B., Harrisburg, Pennsylvania**

You are right, but there is no point in it, particularly if his uncle is no longer living and there is no possibility of confusion. It may be written II or 2d.

## GENERAL INVITATIONS AND REPLIES

**Can you issue a formal invitation on a calling card or just informal ones? How is this done? L.H., Miami, Florida**

You may use your calling card (which should be engraved, of course) to issue *informal* invitations. The card is sent in an envelope it fits exactly or a regular correspondence size envelope. Today, sometimes a joint card is also used for the issuing of invitations, as is the joint informal. On the visiting card carrying a message, you may or may not—as you wish—draw a line through the engraved name if the message is signed informally with a Christian name. For example:

> *Birthday party for Lillian*
> *Saturday, August 9, 5–7*
> ~~Mrs. Henry Eugene Cox~~
> *Do hope you can come.*
> *Love, Julia*

*R.S.V.P.*                    Cold Spring Harbor
                             Long Island

A joint card is used this way,

*Cocktails Sunday*
Mr. and Mrs. Joseph Asa Benet
*Sept. 6th, 4–6*

Bayside Avenue
East Islip, Long Island

✐ ✐ ✐

**Is it considered more correct to write informal invitations or to telephone or give them in person?** Y.H., Charleston, South Carolina

Such invitations may be telegraphed, telephoned, or given in person, as well as by note.

✐ ✐ ✐

**In using a fold-over informal, is it proper to use all of the available writing space or should you limit it to the space opposite the engraved or initialed front—and should you ever write on the back part?** B.W., El Paso, Texas

The informal is designed for brief notes and looks better when it is reserved for that. However, it is not actually incorrect to lay the informal flat and to begin writing at the top and continuing on over to the back section. It would be unattractive to see writing on the front section where your name or initials may appear, if they are put on in such a way as to form a design that dominates that first page. If they are at the top and small then you may, if you wish, begin your note on that first page. The new card informals with a monogram or initials upper left or center or with a name and address engraved in the upper section are meant to have writing on the face. For example:

46 East Fifty-first Street
Mrs. Humphrey Arden Hanshaw
*Tea, Saturday, April 12th*
*4–6*

✐ ✐ ✐

Sometimes my husband and I receive invitations on visiting cards with an R.S.V.P. in the lower left-hand corner. Sometimes they come without an R.S.V.P. when it is for a cocktail party or a tea. In either case what do we do? May we use our own visiting card for a reply? Is it all right to telephone our acceptance or regrets? Mrs. K.P., Wilmington, Delaware

Where there is no R.S.V.P. on a visiting card invitation, the hostess expects you to come if you can. It is not incorrect to let her know that you'll definitely be there. It is pleasant if you don't get there to let her know in some way afterward that you appreciated the invitation. You might even send your card later saying, "Hear the tea was a great success. I wish I could have been there—and thank you. Marie." For such little messages on visiting cards salutation and closing are never used and on informals are not necessary, although the inside of an informal is often treated as if it were note paper. Yes, you may telephone your acceptance or regrets. If you use your calling card or an engraved informal in accepting an informal invitation requiring a reply, you do it this way (in black ink):

*We accept with pleasure for*
*the 6th at eight*
~~Mr. and Mrs. Lawrence Armitage~~
*Lucy*

*Love to come Friday*
~~Miss Laura Sue Ramsey~~
*at five*
*Laura*

If the couple is not on a first-name basis, a line is not drawn through the names on their joint visiting card. As it is the wife who replies to invitations with the example given, she writes in longhand "Lucy," not "Lucy and Lawrence."

✦     ✦     ✦

Is it correct to send out invitations written in pencil or typed out over the hostess's name? Mrs. W.F.M., Dallas, Texas

No, it is not. When invitations are sent they should be handwritten, engraved, or, under certain circumstances, printed. Ink should be used.

↗    ↗    ↗

We are buying a house ten miles from the city we now live in. Would it be proper to send printed cards announcing our new address and phone number to friends we see only occasionally? If we do it, should our child's name be included? Mrs. S.J.S., Waco, Texas

Yes, this is perfectly proper, and you may include the name of your child if you wish. Some people use printed post cards for this purpose, listing all the essential information.

↗    ↗    ↗

I would like to invite a very old friend who knows most of my friends here to my small apartment so she can meet with them before she goes off into another community to live and work. As I have a job, it is convenient for me to entertain only on weekends. Because of this, although I want to be informal, I would like to know how many people are coming. Also I want to know whether I should write informal notes or use cards on which I would write "Reception in honor of Miss ———" C.S., Green Bay, Wisconsin

As most of your friends know your visitor, the nicest thing would be to write small notes saying that you are giving an "open house" for her on Sunday, the ——— of ———, from, say 4 to 8. This way you could say in the note that you would like to know if they actually plan to come; for example, "Will you let me know if you're coming?" It is not usual to use the R.S.V.P. on a card issued for a reception.

## THANK-YOU NOTES

**Just what is a bread-and-butter note?** M.P., New York, New York

A bread-and-butter letter is a letter of thanks written for entertainment overnight or longer. Technically, a bread-and-butter letter may consist of a mere "Thank you for the lovely weekend," written on the face of your visiting card with a line through your title (Mrs., Mr., or Miss and your last name, too, if you are on a first-name basis) but it is better to make it a little more human even when it must be quite brief. It is usually handwritten though if your handwriting is highly illegible it may be typed. Here is a possible example:

Monday

Dear Mildred,
Your party and the entire weekend, as always, were great fun. I enjoyed meeting the Le Beaus and found them just as stimulating as you promised. In fact, just talking to M. Le Beau stirred me to dig out my French grammar again.

Love,
Josephine

✓ ✓ ✓

**When my husband and I go to an elaborate dinner at somebody's house should I write a thank-you note to my hostess? Just when are thank-you notes obligatory?** Mrs. B.L., Richmond, Virginia

A verbal thank-you is enough unless you have been entertained overnight as well. In this case a thank-you note is always obligatory. When a party has been given especially for you, it is very polite to write a thank-you note to your hostess—and actually it is never impolite to do so even when it is not strictly necessary. A thank-you note should always be written when you have received a gift through the mail and do not have the opportunity to thank the sender either by phone or in person. And even when you have made personal thanks it is never impolite to write a note as well. Thank-you notes must always be written for wedding presents, even when the bride has had an opportunity to thank the donor in person. Such notes need not be long and most people understand if there is a time lag of several weeks between the receipt of the gift and the dispatching of the thank-you note. An example of such a note follows:

Tuesday, May 4
(Address, if address is
unknown to your correspondent.)

Dear Aunt Mary,

Bob and I were thrilled with your generous wedding check. As you know, we won't really be able to have a home of our own until he finishes his military training. We have put your check with others we have received in anticipation of the day when we are ready to shop for our furniture. I hope when Bob has his next leave we'll be able to drive over to see you.

With much love,

Helen

✓ ✓ ✓

**Have we gotten clear away from the idea that greeting cards are merely to supplement when a personal greeting is not possible? I refer especially to the sending of printed thank-you cards to guests who have been present at a shower or birthday party and have already been thanked in person at that time. J.A., Albuquerque, New Mexico**

A verbal thank-you is enough, but a note is never amiss. Thank-you cards should never be sent unless they include a written message. Most conservative people do not use them, even this way, but prefer regular stationery or informals, with no "thank-you" imprinted upon them.

✓ ✓ ✓

**My son is being confirmed, and we are having a large reception in his honor. I know he will receive many gifts, and I wonder if it would be proper for us to have a printed thank-you note made up, as his handwriting is very illegible. B.T., Brooklyn, New York**

No, this is not correct. Where your son has had an opportunity at the reception to thank the donors adequately in person, he need not write a note in addition. Where he has not had a chance to thank people this way, he must write a note, although it can be quite brief. Notes of thanks must always be personally written. The fact that he has performed this little courtesy will overshadow the illegibility of his handwriting.

✓ ✓ ✓

I am to be guest of honor at a stork shower. My hostess is a close friend. Is it enough to call her on the phone the next day to thank her for the shower, or should I write her a note? And what about the girls who will give me gifts? W.P.L., Passaic, New Jersey

Verbal thanks are enough, but if you can manage little notes, this is always especially courteous. As your hostess is a close friend whom you presumably see all of the time, it is enough to thank her by phone the next morning—as well as, of course, the day of the shower.

✓ ✓ ✓

I have a nine-year-old daughter and an eleven-year-old son. When they are casually entertained at the homes of their friends, overnight, is it really essential for them to write thank-you notes to the mothers involved? Mrs. J.A.A., Boston, Massachusetts

The word "casually" is your cue here. If they frequently visit back and forth and there is no special entertainment arranged for them, then a proper verbal thanks to the mother of the children they are visiting is enough. But again, a careful mother does train her children to write thank-you notes, and certainly one, occasionally, at least, under these circumstances, is never amiss. A child who is specially entertained at someone's home overnight or longer always writes the mother after his return home.

✓ ✓ ✓

My husband and I received a gift from the company for which he works. The card was signed by the president and the vice-president, whom I have never met. The gift was sent to us both at home. Should I acknowledge it in a personal note, or should my husband just thank these officers personally by calling at their offices? Mrs. B.L.J., Birmingham, Michigan

As the gift was sent to you both at home, you yourself should write a personal note of thanks, addressing it to the president of the firm and saying in the body of the letter that your husband and you both wish to thank him and Mr. X (the vice-president) for their kind thought, etc. You sign it yourself, with your married name in parentheses beneath your social signature. Of course, it would always be correct, in addition, for your husband to thank these executives personally if calling by at their offices would not too greatly disrupt his own routine. If it is a very large organization and he feels that he cannot take the executives' time for these thanks, he can leave word with the secretary for them.

## SPECIAL LETTERS

I live in the suburbs and every once in a while some order I give by mail goes wrong. Just how do you cope with a situation like this —do you telephone the store or write an indignant letter? What I want to get is action. H.G., Bronxville, New York

Just remember that individuals in stores are people, too. They are probably besieged by indignant shoppers. The one who will get service will be the one who writes politely and fully—or who calls on the telephone and is considerate and patient with her complaint. Here is a letter, fully explanatory, and giving full benefit of the doubt. It should get results.

786 Decatur Road
Thomasville, Georgia 31792
April 3, 1967

Nu-Fairbanks Seed Company
400 Bond Street
Richmond, Virginia 23223

Gentlemen:

Your company has always given such excellent service that I regret having a complaint to make now. On June 22 you mailed me a package of grass seed I had ordered and which arrived with the carton open and most of the seed gone. I took the matter up with the post office here, and they informed me that the package had not been properly prepared for mailing, nor had it been insured. As the mistake seems to have been made by your shipping department, I am sure you will make good on the order by having the carton more carefully packed before sending it out to me again. Thank you.

Sincerely,

Jane Doe<br>(Mrs. John Doe)

✓ ✓ ✓

**Like all housewives, I have occasion to write some business letters. Can you give me a simple form that I can follow and that will be more or less foolproof? Mrs. G.N., Sarasota, Florida**

Yes, here is the form:

1212 Main Street<br>Weehawken, N.J. 07087<br>May 4, 1967

R. H. Mabee Co.
1200 Boston Post Road
Westport, Conn. 06882

Gentlemen:
Will you please send me two lounging chairs as advertised in last Sunday's *Times* @ $25.75 each. I enclose my check.

Sincerely, (or Sincerely yours,)<br>Adele Lewis<br>(Mrs. Frank J. Lewis)

## CHRISTMAS CARDS

**My husband is in the service and stationed abroad. I am wondering if it would be considered proper to sign our Christmas cards as always or to omit his name, using only mine and our son's? Mrs. F.S., Jr., Macon, Georgia**

Include him, as always.

✓ ✓ ✓

Do you approve of Christmas cards or greeting cards of any kind being sent second-class mail—that is, with the flap tucked inside the envelope and the envelope unsealed? Mr. D.W., Syracuse, New York

No, any communication with a friend which requires an envelope deserves the dignity of a five-cent stamp.

✓ ✓ ✓

Is it correct to send Christmas cards with the name imprinted, rather than personally signed? A.M.C., Beacon, New York

Most people with large Christmas card mailing lists make things easy for themselves by picking one personal card and having it imprinted or engraved if they do not care to sign each one. Others who have the time and the real interest pick individual cards to suit each friend and of course sign each one of these personally. I, myself, like a personal signature, at least to a close friend, even when the card is engraved or imprinted. I like a little message too when I haven't heard from this particular friend for some time.

✓ ✓ ✓

What's correct if you get a Christmas card from someone to whom you haven't sent one and it comes too late for you to send one of yours so it will arrive in time for the holiday? D.O'C., Houston, Texas

If you have a very personal card that perhaps includes a photograph of your children, send it anyway with a little note on it that indicates, delicately, that your friend was not on your original list. Say, perhaps, "It was so nice to get your card. Our late wishes are just as merry." Of course, it is not necessary to acknowledge a greeting card, but often you want to when you receive one from a friend at a distance whom you can't thank personally on casual encounter. A brief note, a pretty post card—or a suitable return greeting card will thank him for remembering you.

✓ ✓ ✓

When a husband and wife are signing Christmas cards, whose name comes first? A.S., Stratford, Connecticut

The one signing places his or her name second, out of courtesy. Therefore, it would read, "John and Mary Smith" or "Mary and John Smith." However, if the names on the card are imprinted or engraved, the wife's name comes first, and the names are used after the message. Informal names are always used on informal cards. "Mr. and Mrs." is used only on formal cards and there is an increasing tendency away from them.

✓    ✓    ✓

**Occasionally I would like to write to my congressman or representative. Can you tell me how to address them properly? H.C.C., Springfield, Massachusetts**

You are to be congratulated on your public-spirited feeling. Following is a list of personages many people may at one time or another wish to write to. Congressmen and representatives are on the list:

### THE PRESIDENT OF THE UNITED STATES

*For domestically mailed letter, address:*
  The President
  The White House
  Washington, D.C. 20501
*If his wife is included:* The President and Mrs. Adams

*For letter addressed from abroad:*
  The President of the United States
  The White House
  Washington, D.C., U.S.A. 20501

*Letter opening:*
  Mr. President: (*business*)
  My dear Mr. President: (*social*)

*Closing:*
  Respectfully (*business*)
  Very respectfully (*social*)

### UNITED STATES SENATORS AND STATE SENATORS

The Honorable Angelo Cognato
United States Senate
Washington, D.C. 20510

*If wife is included, the form is:*
The Honorable and Mrs. Angelo Cognato
Home address

*Letter opening:*
Sir: (*business*)
My dear Senator Cognato: (*social*)

*Closing:*
Respectfully *or* Sincerely yours

NOTE   A woman is The Honorable Genevieve P. Schuler (always with given name). If husband is included, the form is: Mr. and Mrs. John Schuler, home address. Official invitations read: The Honorable Genevieve P. Schuler and Mr. Schuler.

### REPRESENTATIVES AND ASSEMBLYMEN

The Honorable Lincoln Chadwick
House of Representatives
Washington, D.C. 20515

*If wife is included, the form is:*
The Honorable and Mrs. Lincoln Chadwick
Home address

*Letter opening:*
Sir: (*business*)
My dear Mr. Chadwick (*social*)

*Closing:*
Respectfully *or* Sincerely yours

NOTE   A woman is The Honorable Lucy Butterfield. If husband is included, the form is: Mr. and Mrs. Amos Butterfield, home address. Official invitations read: The Honorable Lucy Butterfield and Mr. Butterfield.

### PROTESTANT CLERGYMEN WITH DOCTOR'S DEGREES

The Reverend Joseph E. Long, D.D.

*If wife is included, the form is:*
The Rev. Dr. Joseph E. Long and Mrs. Long

*Letter opening:*
  Reverend Sir: (*business*)
  My dear Dr. Long: (*social*)

*Closing:*
  Respectfully yours (*business*)
  Sincerely yours (*social*)

### CLERGYMEN WITHOUT DOCTOR'S DEGREES

The Reverend Frank K. Hanson

*If wife is included, the form is:*
  The Rev. and Mrs. Frank K. Hanson

*Letter opening:*
  Reverend Sir: (*business*)
  My dear Mr. Hanson: (*social*)

*Closing:*
  Respectfully yours (*business*)
  Sincerely yours (*social*)

### ROMAN CATHOLIC PRIEST

The Reverend Father James L. Cullen

*Letter opening:*
  Reverend Father *or* Dear Father Cullen:

*Closing:*
  I am, Reverend Father, etc.

### ROMAN CATHOLIC BROTHERS

Brother William Shine

*Letter opening:*
  Dear Brother William *or* Dear Brother:

*Closing:*
  I am, respectfully yours

## ROMAN CATHOLIC SISTERS

Sister Mary Annunciata

*Letter opening:*
Dear Sister:

*Closing:*
I am, respectfully yours

## RABBI WITH SCHOLASTIC DEGREE

Rabbi Nathan Sachs, D.D., LL.D.
Temple Emmanuel
Bridgeport, Connecticut

*If wife is included, the form is:*
Rabbi (*or* Doctor) and Mrs. Nathan Sachs
   (Some prefer Rabbi to *Doctor*)
Home address

*Letter opening:*
Sir: (*business*)
My dear Rabbi (*or* Doctor) Sachs: (*social*)

*Closing:*
Very truly yours (*business*)
Sincerely yours (*social*)

## RABBI WITHOUT SCHOLASTIC DEGREE

Rabbi Harold Schwartz
Beth David Synagogue
New York, N.Y.

*If wife is included, the form is:*
Rabbi and Mrs. Harold Schwartz
Home address

*Letter opening:*
Sir: (*business*)
My dear Rabbi Schwartz: (*social*)

*Closing:*
Very truly yours (*business*)
Sincerely yours (*social*)

## MILITARY FORMS OF ADDRESS

In the modern Army, rank is used in all grades for both men and women in the service.

Doctors in the service have a starting rank of Lieutenant, and common Army usage dictates that they be addressed by this rank, but junior officers are not infrequently called Doctor. Once, however, they reach Captain or above, they are generally addressed socially by the Army title so long as they remain in the Army. Officially they are always addressed by rank.

Chaplains in the Army and Navy are always called, officially and socially, Chaplain, no matter what the military rank. There is no ruling, however, expressed in regulations, which would prevent men from referring to Catholic priests as Father.

Non-commissioned officers are addressed officially by title, i.e., Sergeant for all grades of Sergeants—First Class, Master, Sergeant, etc.—but there is no regulation prohibiting the use of Mister socially.

A Warrant Officer in any branch of the service is called Mister officially and socially.

In the Navy, Commanders and above are addressed socially by their Navy titles. All below that rank are Mister. Properly a Lieutenant Commander is Mister, but recent custom accords him the courtesy title of Commander socially, with his actual status indicated to all by his two and a half stripes.

Any officer in command of a ship, whatever its classification, is Captain for the period of his command, no matter what his usual title may be.

Cadets of the U. S. Military Academy are Mister socially and in conversational references, but Cadet officially.

National Guard and Reserve officers not on active duty do not use their titles socially or in business affairs unless their activities have some bearing on military matters. Whenever the rank is used, the proper designation must follow the name, i.e., ORC or NG.

Socially and in ordinary military use Lieutenant Colonels, Major Generals, Brigadier Generals, and Lieutenant Generals are known as Colonels and Generals, respectively.

Vice-Admirals and Rear Admirals are Admiral.

# TEEN-AGERS

## *Dear Miss Vanderbilt:*

### DATES

I am fourteen but my parents won't permit me to go on a date because they say I'm too young. The boy I like keeps asking me to go out with him, and I have explained I'd like to but I can't. What do you suggest I do? B.J.W., Chicago, Illinois

Talk it over with your parents and see if they can come to some understanding with you in the matter of limited dates with limited hours and specific places to which you are allowed to go.

✦ ✦ ✦

When I take out my girl who is considerably shorter than I and it begins to rain, should I let her carry the umbrella and I walk out in the rain, or should I attempt, in spite of the disparity of our heights, to hold it over her? G.C.G., Battle Creek, Michigan

You hold it over her unless you are so burdened with packages that this seems impossible, in which case she walks under the umbrella and you walk outside of it.

✦ ✦ ✦

I have always been very fussy about my dates and refuse to go out with boys who are unattractive looking. I figure that if I am seen with one of them, more attractive boys will pass me by, figuring I can't do any better. My sister says the idea, though, is to keep in circulation, and any date is better than no date. Who is right? E.H., Easton, Connecticut

Some of the most attractive men I have ever known have been quite homely. One of the things a girl gets to know, in time, is that a handsome man is not necessarily the most attractive escort. If you have been sitting home a lot lately, I would agree with your sister that almost any date is better than none. If you do circulate, you are likely to meet someone in time who will really appeal to you. On the other hand, never accept an invitation from a boy you really dislike, just for the sake of the entertainment he can offer. He is sure to sense your feelings during the course of the evening. Under such circumstances it is always more fun to stay home with a good book.

*    *    *

**Some of the fellows in our neighborhood have a habit of calling up girls they don't know, trying to make blind dates. Sometimes they call me and some of my girl friends, saying they know who we are through fellows in high school. My mother says I should have nothing to do with them, but it seems all right to me. I said I'd ask you. J.W.I., Newark, New Jersey**

Your mother is right. Blind dates are very dangerous unless they are arranged by someone you actually know and can trust. Even then it is safer to take another couple along on a blind date. This way you have some protection in the event of some disagreeable occurrence. Boys who do their blind dating in packs on telephones are usually pretty poor pickings themselves, or they wouldn't have to get dates this way.

*    *    *

**I am a girl fifteen and have started going steady with a boy who is very quiet. Whenever he calls me I have nothing to say to start a conversation. What could I say to him to start a conversation? D.M., Pasadena, California**

First, you're much too young to go steady, but the best way to get a boy to talk is to ask him a question about himself. Most people, especially teen-agers, are only too ready and willing to talk about themselves, whereas it is often difficult for them to talk about impersonal things, especially when a conversation is just beginning. That is why convention has us ask, "How are you?" to which the traditional reply is "Fine, thank you. How are you?" Conversations, like automobiles, have to warm up. Therefore don't be afraid of the tried and true subjects as beginners, such as weather, school activities, sports, etc. Eventually, as young boys and girls get to know each other, they can get into fairly deep subjects, I well remember.

✔   ✔   ✔

**I am a girl of fifteen. My mother says nice girls don't call up boys. I think this has changed, don't you? M.D.S., Phoenix, Arizona**

Yes, it has changed somewhat. A girl should really have some excuse for calling up a boy unless she wants to seem to be chasing him. Perhaps she needs to call him about homework or to invite him to a dance or, under certain circumstances, to some entertainment at her own home. If she knows the boy very well and sees him all the time, she could call him just to talk as she might any other friend, but she should be very careful not to overdo it.

✔   ✔   ✔

**I'm a teen-age boy and I get a lot of calls from a girl I can't stand. Her mother is a friend of my mother's, and my mother says I have to be polite. I say I have a right to go out with the girls I pick and this girl should be made to stop chasing me. What do you say? T.S., Jr., New York, New York**

Perhaps it's the mothers who are to blame, not the girl. Undoubtedly the girl is being told by *her* mother to include you in her various entertainment plans. Perhaps you should accept an occasional invitation, but any girl will get the idea in time that you're not interested in her. It is not necessary that you squire her around on your own initiative, you know. If you don't invite her to go out with you in turn, she'll find another boy who'll enjoy her company for her own sake, not because he's asked by his mother to act as her escort. Of course, mothers should know such machinations are usually most ineffective.

✔   ✔   ✔

**Recently I double dated and afterward the other boy called me up and asked me for a date. My mother says that I shouldn't accept it unless we inform both the other boy and the other girl involved**

**of our intention of going out together. Do you really think this is necessary?** Miss J.E.O., Beloit, Wisconsin

As you met through the boy who took you to the dance, I think it would be good manners for the second boy to ask the first if he minded if he invited you as his own date on the occasion you mention. At the same time, if you know the other girl well, you might ask her if she has any objection to your going out with her previous date. If the two had been dating steadily, your action might otherwise seem like beau-stealing. However, as so much dating is so very casual, very probably neither will object if you two have a date together after having met this way. It is nice to ask, however, but you should be prepared to refuse the date if the other girl is obviously hurt or the boy with whom you went out at first seems upset. If the attraction between you two newly-met young people is very strong, then, of course, later on you probably would date anyhow. It is good manners to be sporting about these relationships even at the most casual stage. Just think how you might feel if the whole situation were reversed.

## RESTAURANT ETIQUETTE

**When I am at a restaurant with a boy, how do I order dinner?** A.M., Houston, Texas

You do not pick up the menu yourself, but you wait until it is presented to you by your escort or by the waiter. You give your order to the escort rather than to the waiter, although if the waiter asks you specific questions about your order you may answer him direct. Let your escort make a few suggestions on what might be nice to eat—he may be thinking painfully of his pocketbook though, rightly, he shouldn't take you to a restaurant where this matters to him. But you, of course, as a considerate person, will not order the most expensive dish unless you know that money is no object. In an unpretentious restaurant or say at a country hotel where the food is all table d'hôte, you would be expected to give your order to the waiter when he asks for it. It is only when a card is presented that you give your order to your escort, for it is his masculine duty to scan the card and suggest things that might appeal to your palate. It is also he who suggests the wine, if any. A girl may know all about food herself, but, as a guest of a man in a restaurant, she defers politely to his suggestions although, of course, she's not required to eat anything that she doesn't like.

*      *      *

When I get taken to a nice restaurant by a date I never quite know what's expected of me once we get inside the door. I feel so lost when my date goes to check his hat. I don't know where to stand, and I don't know whether to go with the headwaiter or waitress if they arrive before my date does from the checkroom. Could you give me explicit advice on this subject? J.O.L., Jefferson City, Missouri

Your feeling of helplessness can be a great social asset in this instance. Just allow your date to take full charge. He probably feels just as unsure as you do, but you mustn't let him know that you know it. If he doesn't escort you out of the line of traffic at the entrance while he checks his hat, you step out of it yourself although you don't follow him. You wait quietly without seeming too interested in your surroundings until he rejoins you, then together you approach the entrance to the dining room. There if the headwaiter or hostess steps forward, your escort should step back and let you follow the individual who is to direct you to your table. If no one does step forward to guide you, then your escort steps in front of you and you follow along until he has found a table and pulled out a chair for you. You allow him to seat you.

*      *      *

At the end of a restaurant meal when a boy and girl are dining together which one indicates that it's time to leave? R.J.H., Boise, Idaho

The girl. She places her napkin unfolded at the left of her plate, looks questioningly at her escort, and then prepares to rise. If he suggests they linger she may do so if she wishes. However, her decision must be abided by.

## DANCES AND PARTIES

We are having a formal dance from nine to twelve **P.M.** and are inviting escorts. Does my escort see that I have a way of getting there or should I? Should I dance every dance with my escort? How often may I go to the powder room? Would it be impolite to leave him to talk to a girl friend? When we go home should I give him my coat so he can help me with it? Do I kiss him good night? Do I thank him for the evening or, since he is my guest, should he thank me? "Anonymous," Chicago, Illinois

Taking your questions in order. Your escort calls for you and gets you home at a time agreed upon with your mother who, I hope, will be waiting up for you. You are not obligated to dance every dance with your escort, but he should not leave you until he sees that you have someone with whom to dance. You go to the powder room as often as necessary—and I mean necessary. You mustn't spend the whole evening in there primping or gossiping. Do not leave your guest to talk to a girl friend, but, if you wish, ask him to accompany you to another group. When it is time to go home you allow him to help you into your coat if he is with you. He doesn't follow you into the girls' dressing room, if there is one, for this purpose. You kiss him good night, briefly, only if you want to. A girl is never obligated to kiss a boy just because he expects it. It is always the boy who thanks the girl for her company, but a girl should always say that she has had a very good time—even when she hasn't.

✓    ✓    ✓

A friend of mine is giving a Sweet Sixteen Party for her daughter. Is it quite all right to invite several friends or aunts of the girl to attend—sort of chaperones, so to speak? The party will be held at a well-known inn. Mrs. M.K., Harrisburg, Pennsylvania

At sixteen, teen-agers usually like to have a minimum of chaperonage, and while the girl's mother of course will be there and standing next to her daughter as the guests come in, I think she should discuss with her daughter whether or not any of her mother's friends or the girl's aunts would be really welcome. Or whether the young people might feel that they would put a damper on the party. Chaperones today, I feel, are still needed but should merely lend an air of security and protection without being omnipresent.

✓    ✓    ✓

**Do you feel that a party of all girls or all boys in their middle teens can be given in the home of one of them in the evening without the parents or some other older person actually being in the house during the whole period?** A.H.S., Boston, Massachusetts

Yes. A chaperone is needed only in mixed groups, under the circumstances. But again, children need the support of their parents in such social situations, and parents should not fail to appear at some time during the evening to greet the guests and lend the feeling of family solidarity.

✓    ✓    ✓

**For years I have wondered what a girl is supposed to say to a fellow after they have danced together and he takes her back to the table. The fellow usually says, "Thank you." Then what does the girl say! I hear that some girls don't say a thing. I usually say, "You're welcome."** Mrs. B. McK., Detroit, Michigan

I think it is nice for girls to show their pleasure under such circumstances—or at least to simulate it. Instead of the trite phrase "You're welcome"—which is correct enough, mind you—I think it is nice for a girl to say in different ways, "I enjoyed it too," and to sound as if she means it. Even a girl who isn't such a very good dancer can make the boy feel so appreciated that he comes back and asks her again in preference to a girl who seems to be doing him a great favor by dancing with him at all.

✓    ✓    ✓

**I go to an all-girl school, and whenever we have a formal or semi-formal dance it is customary for the girls to invite a boy to escort them and take care of all the expenses, with the exception of the tickets. What would you consider proper notice to give a boy when asking him to the dance? I think the possibility of his**

having to earn the money himself should be taken into consideration. Also, can you tell me a pleasant and tactful way of telling a boy what kind of flowers you want? So often they bring a shade that doesn't go with the girl's gown. B.A.J., Pittsburgh, Pennsylvania.

As these dances don't take place very often during the year, you should be able to let the boy know a month or more in advance where you think there might be some problems financially. For ordinary invitations, as you know, two weeks is considered sufficient time. Most boys know that they are expected to send or bring a corsage to the girl they take to a dance, but sometimes they just can't afford it. Therefore, I would hate to have you suggest what kind of flowers you would like to wear. Sometimes another boy or girl can tell your escort what kind of a dress you are going to wear better than you could yourself. Boys going to the same party usually do discuss these problems. In cities and in some schools and communities the girls no longer wear corsages but any girl, of course, loves to receive cut flowers.

✓   ✓   ✓

I have had several friends over to my house for a day or evening. Every time I do so I feel like a boring hostess and that my friends want something to do. Do you know of a way to cure me of this feeling? A.M.P., Fort Worth, Texas

You don't say how old you are, but I assume that you are a teen-ager. Feelings of inadequacy overcome much more mature hostesses from time to time, especially when a party doesn't seem to "jell." I myself love good conversation, but sometimes one does find guests who will not talk readily. For this there is no cure except activity of some kind—dancing, music playing, a record session, cards, or any of the parlor games that are popular in your set. For a young hostess it is always well to have such entertainment quickly available, if not actually planned, for such occasions. Never, however, insist as a hostess that your guests play a game in which they seem on the whole disinterested. Often people have lots of fun doing nothing in particular, just relaxing in each other's company, without strictly planned entertainment or scintillating conversation. You don't have to be "doing something" every minute to have a good time.

✐     ✐     ✐

**I have invited a boy to a junior prom. We are both graduating from junior high school. I hope he is going to send me flowers. Should I get him a boutonniere? If so, what kind and color? Should I give him a graduation present—I think he is giving me one. D.K., San Diego, California**

No, don't give him a present. If he hasn't planned to give you one himself, he might be very embarrassed at receiving one from you. Even if he does give you one, it isn't necessary for you to reciprocate. That's one of the nice things about being a girl—when you receive a gift you are not expected to give one in return to a boy. You usually wait on this until you are engaged. If your escort brings you flowers it is all right to give him a boutonniere from them, but don't order one separately for him. It is best, always, to let the boys take the initiative in this giving business. They like us to be the receivers—I guess because it makes them feel so manly.

✐     ✐     ✐

**Would you help us with this problem? A is having a Sweet Sixteen Party at a night club. B says guests should bring gifts to be opened there. C says it is not a proper place or setting for a gift-opening. What do you say? Mrs. M.G., Jamaica, Long Island**

As gifts are usually brought to birthday parties, I do not see that it makes any difference in this case that the setting is to be a night club.

✐     ✐     ✐

**My boy friend's family entertained me at their home in another part of the state. Would it be all right to send his mother some flowers in thanks? M.D., Pittsburgh, Pennsylvania**

Yes, quite all right and very nice, too.

✐     ✐     ✐

My daughter is giving a dinner party for six before the Junior Assembly. The other boys have called their dates and asked what kind of dresses they're going to wear so they can send corsages. However, my daughter's date has not called her. She's afraid she'll be the only girl at the dance without flowers. Would it be all right for us to get her some flowers and keep them in the refrigerator just in case? W.E., Hartford, Connecticut

That would be a good idea, but keep the flowers very modest—the sort of thing the boy would probably send himself. Perhaps he feels that the safest thing to send, if one doesn't know the color of the girl's dress, is white, and perhaps that's why he didn't ask. In a situation like this, tactful parents or a foresighted girl can save an awkward situation. Perhaps the boy couldn't afford the flowers, even though you are paying for the dance tickets. Perhaps he forgot. But if he appears without flowers he may tell your daughter quietly the real truth—either that he forgot them or, without embarrassment, that he is just squeaking through on his allowance this month and that the flowers will have to wait until next time. At this point your daughter, with perfectly good humor, might say, "As a matter of fact, I have some—so everything's all right."

*    *    *

Do you have any sort of rules for parents regarding teen party behavior? Mrs. W.R.T., Houston, Texas

Yes, here are some excellent ones, circulated by the Parents Association of the Loomis School, Windsor, Connecticut.

1. Insist that your boy or girl go to no party to which he or she is not invited and that none be allowed at your parties who is not invited.

2. Have no parties at your home unless you are there. Every party of teen-agers should be adequately chaperoned.

3. Impress upon your son or daughter the full extent of the responsibility involved when he or she is driving someone in a car.

4. Alcoholic beverages should not be served to boys or girls of high school age.

5. Parties should end at a reasonable hour. Insist that your boy or girl telephone you if he or she is to be out later than agreed or if there are other changes in their plans.

6. Boys should ask the parents of their dates what time the girls are expected home and should comply with the parents' wishes. They should also advise the parents where they are going.

✓ ✓ ✓

**I am twelve years old and am about to have my first big party with boys and girls. At other parties I go to they play kissing games. I know they will expect to play them at my party, but I suppose my mother will object. Do you think kissing games are all right? J.M.L., Tallahassee, Florida**

They are very usual at your age and even later and have been played, one way or the other, by generations of children. I'm very sure your mother knows all about it and played them herself at your age. So long as they stay within the rules of good taste I see nothing wrong with them. Your mother, however, is the final arbiter in the matter, so, if she seriously objects, do substitute something else.

## DRESS

**I have been having an argument with my mother for a long time about my wearing earrings. She said I was too young to wear those button-type earrings, and I say I am not because all the other girls my age wear them. She told me to write you and find out if you think a fourteen-year-old girl is too young to wear earrings. A.S., Waco, Texas.**

You have almost answered this yourself. You say all the other girls your age wear them. Generally, what the others in the group do, so long as these things are not really harmful, can usually be a safe guide to parents. I can't see anything particularly harmful in button earrings at your age, but if they really disturb your mother, why don't you wait a while? I know what she means. She doesn't want you to try to look like a grown-up young lady when you are still only fourteen. She doesn't want you to look in any way "cheap" by using a lot of make-up, tottering around in very high heels, wearing your dresses cut too low. My own mother used to call this "gilding the lily." There's something wonderfully young and fresh about the age of fourteen in a girl, and it is very nice if she just looks fourteen.

*    *    *

**My fifteen-year-old daughter wants to get a very low-necked gown for the junior prom. She says a lot of the other girls are wearing them and that I'm just old-fashioned. Should I stick to my guns? S.K.Q., St. Petersburg, Florida**

Within reason. Some really charming and youthful dresses for that age group have fairly low necks. It's the dark, slinky, siren type of dress that makes a girl that age look as if her mother weren't keeping an eye on her. Your daughter shouldn't be allowed to dress like a woman of the world—although it is hard to convince youth that youth itself is a precious and all too fleeting thing.

*    *    *

**I am twelve years old and four feet eight inches tall. My parents say that I cannot wear lipstick because I am small and too young, but I would like very much to wear lipstick. They think I should wait a few years. What do you think? M.F., Fair Lawn, New Jersey**

I hate to see girls of your age wearing lipstick, but I know that in some communities girls as young as you wear pale lipstick to parties at least. If this is the case in your community, maybe you can get your parents to compromise and let you wear it only under certain circumstances.

*    *    *

**I am twelve and a half and would like to know if I may wear nylons. All of my friends wear them to parties and such. M.K.J., Oak Park, Illinois**

Yes, I think you are old enough to wear nylons to parties if the other girls do. Actually I think socks are much prettier, though, especially as girls so young as yourself usually don't fill out the nylons very well, and they tend to bag over the knees. As teen-agers love to wear socks of various kinds, I don't see anything too little-girlish about your wearing socks, even to parties, at your age.

✓        ✓        ✓

I am a girl fifteen years old. I have been invited to a football game by a boy and to dinner after the game. May I wear a suit and go without a hat? Should I change if we go out to dinner afterward? I never wear a hat except to church on Sunday. A.F.S., Indianapolis, Indiana

A wool suit would be proper—a tailored one. A topcoat or a fur coat, if you have one, to keep you warm would be advisable, too. You may go without a hat, both during the game and afterward. Ask your escort his plans for after the game. Probably he will take you to some restaurant where the crowd goes in their football costumes. It is unlikely too that he would want to have to go home to change.

✓        ✓        ✓

I am sixteen and am going to have my first tuxedo. My father is holding out for the usual black but I would like to have midnight blue. He thinks that's just a fad and that I'll be sorry, but we agreed to abide by your decision. C.C., Oakland, California

Midnight blue for tuxedos is no fad but has been an established fashion for some seasons now. It looks blacker than black at night, and you are much more likely to outgrow your tuxedo than to outgrow the fashion for midnight blue.

✓        ✓        ✓

There's going to be a dance at our school this winter. I wonder if it is proper to wear a nile green paper taffeta dress with nile green shoes to match. There are many girls waiting for your kind answer. H.B., Newtonville, Massachusetts

Yes, the dress is very suitable. In almost any season delicate colors are quite appropriate for party dresses, especially for young girls.

✓        ✓        ✓

Would it be proper to wear a pastel-colored lace dress (and shoes to match) to a dinner and dance at a hotel in November? I have been told it isn't appropriate at that time of year. M.S., Newark, New Jersey

Yes, it is appropriate. In fact, lace is now an all-year-around fashion. It is quite proper to wear matching shoes.

## INTRODUCTIONS AND GREETINGS

My mother has a different name than my own because she's been married twice. When I bring my friends home, should I just say, "John, this is my mother," or should I say, "John, this is my mother, Mrs. Barclay." B.S.J., Tacoma, Washington

The latter is correct. Otherwise, the guest might be embarrassed by calling your mother by your name and then finding out later that he has misaddressed her.

✦   ✦   ✦

I live in an apartment hotel where many older ladies live. Should I, a high school senior, stand if they happen by, standing briefly to greet me or for an informal chat while I am dining? Also when girls my own age are arriving and leaving at a party, shall I then arise? Please tell me also if a teen-age girl (eighteen) should curtsy. K.C., Battle Creek, Michigan

Yes, at your age it is courteous for you to rise for women very definitely older than yourself—women in the category, say, of your mother's friends. You would not have to rise for young marrieds. At a party, unless you are a hostess or a member of the family, it would not be necessary for you to rise when other women guests are coming or going. At your age you should definitely not curtsy— in fact I'm against the curtsy for all except little girls who move perhaps in the diplomatic set or who just love to curtsy. Of course in dancing school the curtsy is *de rigueur,* and should be.

✦   ✦   ✦

So few parents seem to be teaching their sons to stand up when lady guests enter a room that I am wondering if I am old-fashioned in teaching my son to do so. Also, do the men rise when friends greet us while we are eating in a booth? A.C.W., Oakland, California

You are right, of course. Parents should teach their sons this essential of etiquette just as early as they are able to absorb the information. Boys should also stand when male guests enter the room, even their own contemporaries, and come forward to greet them with a friendly handshake. They should rise, too, for their fathers returning home after a day's work. No, the men do not rise when they are seated in a booth, although they may half rise and make apologies for not fully rising. However, no lady ever lingers unless she can seat herself quickly so as to prevent the men's discomfort.

❧  ❧  ❧

I am fourteen. How do I introduce boys and girls at a party. Do you mention the last names? A.D., Indianapolis, Indiana

You say, mentioning the girl first, "Sue, this is Joe Adams, Joe, Sue Clarke." In introducing two boys, say, "Joe—Bill Burke, Bill, Joe Adams." Always try to add something to an introduction that will help the two start a conversation. For example, "I think you were both at the Scout Jamboree in New Hampshire last year."

## GIFTS

I am in high school and have been going with a boy for about a year. Would it be all right to give him a white shirt and tie for his birthday? "Patty," Duluth, Minnesota

Well, the shirt I would consider too personal, but the tie is permissible these days. Other possible gifts would be a sweater, socks, you have knitted yourself, gloves, scarf, or handkerchiefs.

❧  ❧  ❧

I have been dating a boy steadily for seven months. I have been over to his house for dinner, and I also have been in the family's company quite frequently. Is it proper for me to give something to his parents at Christmas? And perhaps to his brother and his brother's girl, at whose house I have been a guest several times? And my parents want to know whether they should give my boy friend a gift. D.B., Bronx, New York

It would be quite normal for you and the young man to exchange Christmas presents. I do not advise, however, that you give to the others you mentioned or that your family give a gift to the young man.

✓ ✓ ✓

I know you advise that gifts should not be accepted unless one is engaged; that is, expensive gifts. While vacationing I dated a fellow who was introduced through a personal friend. He visited my family and took me out quite often. At the end of my vacation he brought me a "going away" gift, a costume jewelry bracelet, which I know must have cost at least twenty-five dollars. I accepted it rather than hurt his feelings. Was I in error? T.D., Harrisburg, Pennsylvania

No, costume jewelry does not come within this ban. An unengaged man should not give to a girl such things as real diamonds, pearls, or mink coats. He must avoid anything so personal as underthings. A recent news picture showed an important American diplomat, fastening on his daughter's wrist a large rhinestone bracelet which, it was explained, was a "gift from one of her boy friends." So, you see, gifts of costume jewelry are quite all right, even though the cost is sometimes as high as that you mention. After all he could also have sent you a large spray of orchids that could have cost the same amount of money or entertained you at an equally expensive dinner.

✓ ✓ ✓

I have a class ring I got from a boy in grammar school. Now we are both in high school, and, although we date occasionally, it really doesn't mean anything to me anymore. Should I give it back to him or just not wear it and say nothing? V.S., Detroit, Michigan

Give it back to him, and say something about how much fun it was wearing it but that you feel you don't want to wear anything like that now. He'll understand.

## LITTLE COURTESIES

**In bad weather, when girls have to wear storm boots to parties, should the boys help them off and on with them? M.I.S., Portland, Maine**

Yes, especially if these are removed out-of-doors, on the porch, or in a lobby. If the girls have a separate dressing room where they are asked to remove their outer things, they manage their storm boots by themselves. And a girl who has removed her storm boots in the dressing room doesn't appear with them helplessly in her hand, at departure time, to get her escort's assistance. If he is something less than crazy about her he may consider her just a nuisance at a moment when he has many things to think of himself—making his adieux, collecting his own belongings, getting the car, etc.

✓ ✓ ✓

**My brother was visiting us and was ready to leave when I asked my eighteen-year-old daughter to get her uncle's coat. She replied that a girl does not get a man's coat, that he should go and get it himself. Is it proper for a girl to hand the male guests their coats, whether they are friends or relatives? Mrs. M.A.C., West Orange, New Jersey**

As your assistant hostess she may properly get a male visitor's coat. If you were alone and had male visitors you would be likely to at least make the gesture of opening the closet door and getting out the coat, although you would not necessarily help a man into it. Even when she is much older, if there is no acting host in the household to perform such a function for male guests, she will be the one to make this slight gesture of farewell. Like you, too, she also rises to welcome her guests, male or female, and again rises to see them off.

✓ ✓ ✓

My family isn't poor, but we come from a neighborhood you couldn't exactly call fancy. My mother was careful to teach us good manners, but I guess they aren't the same manners other people expect sometimes from a fellow. Recently I began going around with a girl who lives in a big apartment house on the other side of town. She says I embarrass her sometimes—like the time I got out of the cab and helped her out in front of her house. She said I should have let the doorman do it. How can I learn? J.B.M., Springfield, Massachusetts

Your girl, young like yourself, is just learning, too, or she wouldn't be so sensitive. It would never occur to me to be offended if my escort chose to escort me out of a cab while the doorman stood by. Usually, where there is a doorman, it is more convenient for him to perform this service while the gentleman pays the taxi driver. Also, this is the doorman's function, and he may be jealous of it. Certainly, when he is busy with many other passengers, you would help your girl out of the cab rather than keep her and the cab waiting. As for learning, read etiquette material and ask your girl. Women love to teach manners and are flattered by being asked what's right.

✓     ✓     ✓

I am sixteen and have a friend who hasn't been taught things concerning cleanliness at home. I feel, as her most intimate friend, I should try to help her along these lines. But when I approach her it seems I am too blunt and she is hurt. How should I bring up this tender subject? P.C.I., Little Rock, Arkansas

Don't—in so many words. Put yourself in your friend's place. You wouldn't like to be told that you needed a manicure, that your hair could do with more frequent shampooing, that your shoulder straps are soiled. In telling your friend these things, no matter how kind your intentions, you make her feel inferior and resistant to your advice. Instead, why not suggest that you do some of these things together? Ask her to give you a shampoo and help you with your hair, and you do the same for her. Give yourselves manicures together and perhaps ask her to help straighten up your bureau drawers. Make her feel that she does know these things, and you will find that she will take pains to acquire any knowledge that

you can so tactfully give her without seeming to preach. Learning
these things at your age can be a lot of fun—and beau-catching,
too. Your friend is sure to find that out and want desperately to
be as attractive as possible.

✓     ✓     ✓

My teen-age son often comes home from various public places
with ash trays he has taken as souvenirs. He tells me all the
other boys and girls his age do likewise. I tell him that no matter
what they do it is still stealing, and I won't permit him to keep
these things in his room. He thinks me unreasonable. Do you
agree? Mrs. T.S.C., Butte, Montana

I think *he* is unreasonable. The purloining of other people's prop-
erty is stealing. However, some restaurants and night clubs do
expect a certain amount of this "lifting" of such things as ash
trays, and they consider it good advertising for these things to be
taken out of clubs and into people's homes. If a boy or girl
wishes to have one of these things with the name of the public
place upon it and asks permission to take it, that is another thing.
Just be sure how your son came by these articles. Anything not
honorably come by should be taken back—or if necessary, sent
back with a note of apology.

✓     ✓     ✓

I am a boy in boarding school. I love to get letters, of course,
especially from girls. When I meet them on vacations, is it all right
to ask them to write to me, or do I have to write to them first?
J.O'N., Rowayton, Connecticut

You should ask them if you may write to them, and then you
write the first letter and hope they'll answer you. Girls, by the
way, should not write to boys in boarding school without being
asked to do so, unless there's some very good reason, such as the
tendering of an invitation.

✓     ✓     ✓

I know that it is not necessary for men or boys to remove their
hats in public buildings such as stores or office buildings. I do
wonder, however, if a school building would be considered public
in the same sense as a store? Mrs. E.B., Morristown, New Jersey

Since a school is a place for learning, it should be a place where boys are taught good manners. For this reason they should remove their hats upon entering, even though a school may be considered a public building.

## SPECIAL PROBLEMS

My son has had an allowance since he was six, and I think he's handled it very well. Now he is fifteen, and he would like me to increase his allowance so that he can buy all of his own clothes, and perhaps even have a checking account. Do you think this is wise? Mrs. F.O.M., Wichita, Kansas

It depends very much on the boy, but your boy sounds as if he could stand the increased responsibility. It would be valuable to teach him now how to handle a checking account. He might open a special account in your local bank—and, at his age, it is permissible. He must learn the responsibility of handling his money well, of never overdrawing, of keeping careful account of what he spends and of what he deposits. Certainly, fifteen is not too early to learn this. If you can, go back with him over your own accounts and determine what you have been spending a year for his clothes, and then add something to it for the future year when he will be growing and needing, perhaps, more clothes for social things. You can then arrive at the amount he needs for school, for spending money, and for clothes. If he is the kind of boy you describe, I think that he could well manage this whole sum given to him once, or, divided, twice a month. It should be put into his checking account, and he should pay his bills himself. An arrangement like this obviates the many arguments the mothers and fathers of teen-agers have as to whether or not a boy or girl may have a certain article of clothing he desires. The answer is, "If you can afford it out of your allowance and nothing else suffers seriously, by all means, use your judgment and get it if that seems important."

✐　　✐　　✐

My daughter is sixteen years old and is a junior in high school. She would like to go to a private school. I have not had a college education, and I shall have to meet the head of the school for an interview. Do you suppose I will hinder my daughter's chances of being accepted at the school? I know if I had the social background, she would have no difficulty in being accepted. I have a friend who has several degrees and who is now doing research work at one of the foremost universities. He has gone to private schools all his life. Wouldn't it be better for him to go with my daughter when she visits the school? I myself am a widow. M.A.S., Orange, New Jersey

Your friend's educational background has nothing to do with the desirability of your daughter as a student in the school to which you want to send her. In all good private schools, children come from all sorts of backgrounds in this country and from abroad. You do not have to have a college education to be a well-informed and attractive person. I am sure your daughter is proud of her mother and wants you to go with her. Surely the school would prefer it that way. The top schools, of course, have rigorous scholastic requirements and more or less pick and choose among children they think will represent the school well. They are interested in character and genuine social attractiveness, rather than in family background and the social position of the family. An attractive boy or girl, with adequate marks, who has something within himself to offer, has the best chance.

✓ ✓ ✓

A few weeks ago I was invited to my boy friend's home. While there I was invited to stay overnight and did so. My parents say this is wrong. What do you think? Would it make any difference if we were engaged? M.M.M., Independence, Missouri

I assume that you were properly chaperoned by the boy's parents and that you, of course, phoned home to ask your parents' permission to stay there and that the boy's mother spoke to your mother. All of these points of etiquette in order, there should be no problem for your parents concerning this invitation that you accepted. You could accept it in this way, even though you were not engaged. You may also invite the boy to your house under the same circumstances.

*          *          *

**This year I am going to an all-girls' school. I have never attended one before and I am having quite a time convincing my friends that I want to go. They think I will miss out on a lot of activities and boy and girl relationships. I tell them that I will have plenty of time for that later. How can I convince them that I really want to go without hurting anybody's feelings and that it is not as bad as they think?** N.N., Seattle, Washington

It seems to me that *you're* the one who is worried, rather than your friends. I myself went to boarding school, but in Europe, where even the holidays did not mean that I would return to my former friends. For many children good boarding schools mean increased concentration on work and often better marks, and social life, when it comes, is enormously appreciated. Often, actually, boys and girls away at school enrich their friendships, not only in their new environment but with those left behind, through correspondence. And such a child coming back on school holidays has the advantage of a certain prestige over those who continue to go to school locally. And when they do come home they seem to be almost fresh, new personalities in their groups because of their absence. This may mean that a girl or boy who didn't have too much success with the opposite sex before going away to school comes back with a glamor that makes previously indifferent friends eager for his attention.

# BABIES AND CHILDREN

## *Dear Miss Vanderbilt:*

### CHRISTENINGS

We are going to have a home christening for our baby. Should formal invitations be sent out? We plan to have it at five o'clock and follow it with a buffet supper. Should both the minister and his wife be invited or just the minister? Isn't there some traditional punch that is served? I.W.R., Long Beach, California

Formal invitations are not sent for a christening. Close friends and relatives are invited by telephone, by word of mouth, and by note. The clergyman's wife is included in the invitation. The traditional drink at christenings was a caudle cup (a mixture of wine or ale with eggs, sugar, and spices), but this has, in the main, been replaced by champagne, plain or in a delicate punch. Often at afternoon christenings a dry sherry is served. It should be kept in mind that this is a celebration in honor of the baby, following a formal religious ceremony. It has a character quite different from a cocktail party and should be kept on such a plane that even the most conservative baby could not object to the behavior and bearing of his elders.

$\checkmark$ $\checkmark$ $\checkmark$

At what age is a baby christened, and is it permissible for male children to wear christening dresses? U.S.Y., Detroit, Michigan

It depends upon the denomination. The matter should be discussed with your clergyman. You should know that some Prot-

estant denominations permit home christenings but that Catholics
do not, except in cases of dire emergency. Some Protestant denominations do not permit christening or baptism until the child
has reached an age of understanding. The Baptists, for example,
have a dedication of babies, but actual baptism usually does not
take place until about the child's tenth year, and of his own free
will. Yes, a boy may wear a christening dress too.

✓     ✓     ✓

**Is it proper to have a grandparent for a godparent in the
Presbyterian church? Do the parents ask the prospective godparents whether they wish to serve before the baby's arrival or
shortly thereafter? Mrs. J.R.L., Louisville, Kentucky**

Although relatives do often serve as godparents, I do not recommend the choice of grandparents as godparents. Godparents should
be the approximate age of the child's actual parents or younger,
because the association with the child should run at least through
his formative years. The godparents have the implied responsibility
of parenthood should the actual parents die before the child
reaches maturity, even though legal guardian arrangements are
usually noted in wills.

Among Presbyterians, baptism (the proper term for this denomination) is one of the two sacraments. However, godparents
are not usually appointed but may be if the parents so desire.

## CHOOSING A NAME

**A fine Irish name for a boy is "Florence." It has long been in
our family, and I would like my daughter-in-law to give it to her
first son in order to maintain the family tradition. She says that
"Florence" is a girl's name in this country and that she would
be handicapping a son by using it, tradition or no tradition. What
do you think? F.A.O'N., Roanoke, Virginia**

I feel that practicality should come ahead of tradition. "Florence"
is not a fighting name for a boy in Ireland, but it well could be
here. Giving a boy a name that could be mistaken for a girl's

name is to put him at a psychological disadvantage. There are so many handicaps to overcome on the way up to adulthood, why add one more in a name?

✓    ✓    ✓

**I want to name my baby for my mother-in-law, if it's a girl. Should she be called "Junior"?** A.J.R., Miami, Florida

No. A girl is never called "Junior," which is a masculine suffix.

✓    ✓    ✓

**If my coming baby is a son we should like to name him for his grandfather. However, my husband had a brother who was named for his father and was therefore "Junior." This brother is mentally ill and will never recover. He is institutionalized. Would it be proper for us under the circumstances to call the new baby "Junior?"** A.G.L., Indianapolis, Indiana

You could not possibly call the baby "Junior" for two reasons. One is that even though his uncle is in a mental institution he still retains his identity, and you may not take it from him. Secondly, "Junior" means "the son of," and your baby will not be the son of his grandfather, obviously. If he is a boy you may call him, however, "Second," naming him for his grandfather.

✓    ✓    ✓

**If my coming baby is a boy I want to name him for my husband who is not a "Junior." Some people tell me "Junior" is old-fashioned and not used anymore and the numeral "II" is correct. I'd appreciate your advice.** R.F.H., Cedar Rapids, Iowa

The term "Junior" actually means "son of." Therefore the child of a father who receives the same name as his father is "Junior." However, if the child is to be named for his grandfather (whose name differs from his father's), he cannot be "Junior" but he is "II" or "2nd." The same is true if he is named for an uncle or a cousin who bears exactly the same name in full, or, if he is named for a very illustrious ancestor, in which case he may be known as "II" or "2nd," "III" or "3rd," or "IV" or "4th," depending on how many others still living are named exactly for that ancestor.

So therefore the term "Junior" is not in any way old-fashioned although there is a trend away from it, fortunately, but it must be used correctly. I prefer to see a child, even when named for his father, have some portion of his name belonging to him alone, either in the first name or the middle name, so that he does not have to be called "Junior" or "little John" the rest of his life— or at least while his father is alive. This is something he may grow to resent.

## BIRTH ANNOUNCEMENTS

My husband and I have been married seven years and are adopting our first baby. It will be one of the happiest moments when he arrives. Could my husband pass out cigars to his co-workers and friends? Our other problem is that we live in a small community, and the arrival will be announced in the local paper. How can it be stated properly and yet made to sound as if he were born to us? Mrs. F.H.H., Cheshire, Connecticut

Of course your husband may pass the cigars, but you should be perfectly frank about the baby's being adopted. You may announce his adoption by sending individual notes to friends and relatives, but you may also have a card engraved. Here is one suggested way of doing it:

*Dr. and Mrs. Arthur George Adamson*
*take pleasure in announcing that*
*Bruce McKay Adamson*
*born on the sixth of June, 1966*
*has been adopted as their son.*

Eighteen Fox Lane
Red Hook, New York 12571

Please do something like this and do not pretend to anyone that you have borne this child yourself, for in the years to come he will certainly happen upon the deception.

✓ ✓ ✓

I am to have a baby in the near future. Of course I want to send out birth announcements, and I am just not sure to whom to send them. Also, there was a surprise baby shower for me. Is it necessary for me to send announcements to all the families that were present? G.K.C., Augusta, Georgia

Stationery stores have very charming little birth announcements which are quite proper to send out. I would send one, if you are sending them, to the various girls who came to the shower for you. A more formal—and more expensive—way of announcing the new baby is to have tiny calling cards with the baby's name attached to your own calling card with white, pink, or blue ribbon. Any good stationer will show you how this is done.

## BABY-SITTERS

How old do you think a baby-sitter should be? Some of my friends employ girls of eleven and twelve to sit with their babies in the evening. I don't think this is right, do you? B.B.T., Pough-keepsie, New York

A child of twelve or perhaps thirteen during the daytime might be satisfactory as a baby-sitter if she is truly responsible and if the mother is within hailing distance. She might be employed to go along with the mother shopping to help with a small child, too. But for evening sitting an older person should take care of a child, especially a tiny baby. A boy or girl in the late teens, known to be stable, conscientious, and really fond of children, would be suitable. For overnight or longer periods, children should be left with an older woman if possible. Sometimes a man and his wife are an even better choice if the house is in an isolated district. A mother should always consider that an emergency might occur with which an immature person might not be able to cope.

✓   ✓   ✓

Do you think that teen-age girls should be allowed to have their boy friends in while they are baby-sitting? L.J.D., Pelham, New York

No, I do not. Baby-sitting is a serious business, and the person taking on this responsibility should not have anything else on her mind. Wise parents do not permit their teen-age daughters to entertain their boy friends when there are no adults in the house. A very responsible girl might be permitted occasionally to have another girl visit her while she is sitting, but she should not be allowed to have a party or, as I have said, to have in boy friends.

## CLOTHES

**Can you suggest some suitable baby presents aside from the usual sacques, bonnets, blankets, etc.? R.R.W., Charleston, West Virginia**

One of my own favorites is that silver dumbbell which makes a fine comfort when the baby's teeth come in. Every baby is enchanted, too, by the wide variety of nursery mobiles now being offered. Hung above the crib, they fascinate him for hours on end. For the infant who is literally going to get "everything," there is nothing better than a savings bond or a contribution to his savings account.

**How soon before a baby is expected should a baby shower be given? Who should give a shower? Mrs. L.M., Norwalk, Connecticut**

Baby showers are usually given about one month before the baby is expected. A shower may be given by a friend of the mother-to-be, never by a relative. Shower gifts may be in neutral colors—white, green, or yellow, or in the traditional pink and blue now worn interchangeably by boys and girls.

## PARTIES

**I am having a graduation party for my son at our home. I am inviting forty people or more, mostly relatives. The relatives have**

small children—some eighteen of them—and usually take them along when they are invited out. Certainly on this occasion I would like the grown-ups to enjoy themselves without worrying about the children. How can I word my invitations, telling them not to bring the children, and yet not offend? Y.M.A., Chicago, Illinois

Tell them just as you have told me. Say that there will be so many coming that if the children come too there will hardly be room for the grown-ups, and ask them if on this occasion they will make arrangements to leave their children at home. If this seems really difficult, perhaps one relative can arrange to take all eighteen, with several sitters, paid for out of a common fund, so that the grown-up party may proceed happily.

*        *        *

In a few months, I expect to become a grandparent. I have been asked to give a baby shower for my daughter. I have declined, simply because I don't think it is proper to give a shower before the birth—so many unfortunate things could happen. Mrs. E.R., Orange, New Jersey

I agree with you only in part. Showers are usually given before the baby's birth, because we do look on the coming event with optimism—which is good and normal. However, you are right in another respect. Arrangements for the shower—any shower, as a matter of fact—should not come from within the family. The shower proposal should come from friends of the mother-to-be, otherwise it looks as if the family itself is soliciting presents for the newcomer. I know you will be able to put this tactfully to those you think should be the sponsors.

## SPECIAL PROBLEMS

My first baby was born dead. Friends gave me many gifts in anticipation of his birth, and now I don't know whether I should return the gifts or what I should do. G.S.N., Princeton, New Jersey

The use of the word "first" in your letter to me indicates what most women know in their hearts—that they will try again after such a tragic circumstance. Do not return the gifts, as this would sadden your friends. Keep them in the hope of having another baby soon.

*   *   *

**When I take my baby shopping, I leave his carriage in the sun outside of the supermarket. Often when I come out I find some strange woman leaning over him, disarranging his blanket, breathing in his face, and, in general, trying to entertain him. I don't like strange people to touch my baby, but I don't know how to say so without being rude. Can you suggest something? Mrs. B.T., Miami Beach, Florida**

I can think of almost nothing you can't say so long as you say it politely and with a pleasant look on your face when an admonition must be made. I would say to such a person, "I'm trying to get the baby to go to sleep, and I hope you don't mind but I'd rather you wouldn't disturb him in any way." Then if she's someone who really can't understand even this and continues to hover over the baby, say, "It's really not very sanitary to put your face so close to a small baby. I never allow it." If you can remember when you have to say something like this that the person who has been attracted to the baby has a tremendous need for maternal expression, you will say what you have to say in the most kindly, yet firm manner. She doesn't really mean to make a nuisance of herself.

*   *   *

**I have a little girl who shuffles as she walks. I have tried everything to get her to pick up her feet but it does no good. What can you suggest? Mrs. J.A.F., Springfield, Missouri**

First, check your doctor to be sure there is no medical reason for this condition. If there is none, check your daughter's shoes. Be sure that her shoes fit properly. If she is wearing loafers, be sure they are not so wide they slip off her feet as she walks. Properly fitting shoes should correct this. You should also tell her that "Ladies never shuffle as they walk but pick up their feet gently and walk straight ahead, toes straight." A shuffling walk is irritating to hear and most unattractive to observe; tell her. Explain that movie stars must all learn to walk beautifully.

*    *    *

I have a son who has a nervous habit of clearing his throat every few minutes. What can I do? Mrs. L.O.N., Wichita Falls, Texas

There may possibly be a medical reason for this. If you've checked your doctor and there is none then at a moment when he seems fairly relaxed, explain to him what he is doing. He is probably quite unconscious of it.

*    *    *

My daughter has a little friend at school who comes from a decidedly underprivileged home. The child comes here often and seems to appreciate it. From time to time she invites my daughter to her home, but as her mother has many other children and they have so little money, I feel this is an imposition, and I don't allow my daughter to accept. However, I am worried about this because obviously the little girl wants to show her appreciation. What should we do? Mrs. D.D., Denver, Colorado

Let your daughter go. Perhaps in this household full of children, the mother has more to give than many more privileged people—financially—imagine. You can help your daughter to maturity by letting her understand that parental love is not dependent upon a bank account, that security is not definitely determined by how one lives, in a material sense.

Can you give me a list of the important "don'ts" that might serve as a guide for my two boys, aged eight and ten? E.S., Cheyenne, Wyoming

Well, they don't:—
  1. Scratch, pick the teeth, spit, comb the hair, or tend the nails in public.
  2. Chew with their mouths open or with obvious noise or lip-smacking.

3. Leave a spoon in a cup, or eat with a knife, or tuck in their napkins, or suck their fingers instead of wiping them on a napkin.

4. Sit down to a meal unwashed and uncombed or improperly dressed.

5. Fail to greet others in the household when they arise or return home.

6. Tilt chairs or lounge on the dinner table or put their elbows on it, except between courses (and then preferably one elbow at a time, if any).

7. Go up and down stairs like elephants and bang doors after them.

8. Pass in front of others without excusing themselves.

9. Use a flat "Yes" or "No" in answer to questions. Instead, "Yes, Mother," or "Yes, Mr. Roberts (or Sir)."

10. Swear in a way that is considered offensive (though most children need a list of acceptable "swear words"—perhaps one list for use in the parents' presence, another list for away from home where there is likely to be more rigidity in the matter).

11. Put more than a manageable mouthful in their mouths at one time.

12. Burp, sneeze, or cough without attempting to turn away from others, and then only behind the cupped hand or a clean handkerchief.

13. Behave noisily and conspicuously in public places.

14. Enter a room whose door is closed without knocking and waiting for permission to enter.

15. Interrupt a conversation except for an important reason and then only after asking permission to speak.

*    *    *

**I am constantly appalled at the atrocious manners exhibited by today's children. They seem to have no regard whatever for the comfort or sensitivities of others. Is this the result of the so-called "permissive" method of upbringing? I don't think much of it. Mrs. E.T.R., Lancaster, Pennsylvania**

I feel that basically children's manners are really absorbed from their parents. This does not mean that I think children should be permitted to be rude or unmannerly as a result of outside influences without having it called to their attention. There are certain accepted manners which children should be continually encouraged to cultivate. They should learn that mother and father do certain things to be socially agreeable and that these courtesies will be expected of them, too, as soon as they are able to cope with them. I have never seen a child with well-mannered parents who grew into an adult completely devoid of social grace. But I have seen such a child, in rebellion at constant goading about his manners, go through a savage period during which the only conformity with social customs was enforced with damaging tension to both child and parents. Such a nagged child gets to believe he *is* a boor and that nothing can remedy the fact, so he might as well be as primitive as possible just to show them. Most children eventually rise to the social graces in their own good time. In the meantime, they should hear us deliver the courteous phrases for them, without irritation. And they need to be told quietly, before and after social events, what will be expected of them as a matter of course.

# BUSINESS ETIQUETTE

## *Dear Miss Vanderbilt:*

### INTRODUCTIONS

I am a secretary who works for two men. We all work in one office. Is it correct for my bosses to introduce me to an outside visitor? Recently we had a visitor from England who spent an afternoon with my bosses. He sat not more than three or four feet away from me. I felt embarrassed at not being introduced, particularly when they left the room and I was alone with him. What do you think? J.M., Detroit, Michigan

Yes, you should have been introduced to him. In a case like this, which concerns business, a subordinate woman worker is introduced to a male superior. Socially, of course, a man is always introduced to a woman.

I am an office manager. When a new secretary comes in, do I introduce her to the other girls on the staff or vice versa? How do I introduce her to the non-executive men, to the executives? B.K., San Francisco, California

In introducing the new secretary to the other girls in the office, you may say, "Miss Brown, this is Miss Smith, who will work with us here in this department now. Miss Smith, this is Miss Brown." In introducing her to her male co-workers, not her superiors, you introduce the men to her, saying, "Miss Smith, this is Mr. Jones, who operates the Comptometer." In introducing her to executives, male, you say, "Mr. Wittlesey, this is (or "I'd like to present") Miss Smith, our new secretary." The new girl rises on being introduced to superiors, male or female.

## CARDS

**When a business firm has cards engraved for Christmas, is it proper to send them to a business associate's home, addressed to husband and wife, or should they be sent to the associate's office, addressed to him alone?** Mr. W.C., Chicago, Illinois

They should be sent either to his home or to his office, addressed to him alone, unless there has also been some business connection with his wife. If the wife has, on occasion, been entertained with her husband by the firm's executives, it would be proper for the firm to include her in the greetings. The card would then be sent home.

*✓ ✓ ✓*

**If a man or woman has a degree which he is entitled to use in his profession, how is it used on his business card and how socially? How does he sign his name in business and how socially?** P.C., Staten Island, New York

Clergymen, doctors of medicine (or allied sciences such as psychology and dentistry), judges, senators, mayors, military or naval officers, governors, professors who make teaching their profession and are holders of university professorships, all use their titles on their social and professional cards. Regarding the doctorates; the letters indicating the title follow the name on the business card, for example: LL.D., M.D., D.D.S., and so forth. Holders of purely honorary degrees usually omit them on both social and professional cards. And, although they may be called doctor, socially, they do not use their degrees in social signatures or on engraved announcements or invitations. A doctor signs himself in business correspondence "John Jones, M.D.," where his social signature is merely "John Jones." But he may use social stationery that carries his title "Doctor John Jones," or even "Dr. John Jones," with his address at the top.

✔    ✔    ✔

How does a man's business card differ from his social card? There are many occasions on which I am never sure whether I should send my business card. For example, if I have a customer who is sailing for Europe and I want to send him flowers, do I send my business card or my social card? Of course, I send the flowers for business reasons. W.F., Richmond, Virginia

You know, of course, the main difference between a man's social card and his business card is that his social card always carries "Mr." before his name, his business card does not. His business card is larger than his social card, and for an executive it is always engraved or printed in black conservative type faces or script. Business cards used for advertising purposes may be printed or engraved in colors, but those of the top executives of the company shouldn't be. In sending flowers under the circumstances you give, you send your social card, as you are making a social gesture on a social occasion. But if the man doesn't know you and your connection with the firm you wouldn't intrude upon him at such a time. On the other hand, if he were opening a new store you could certainly send flowers accompanied by your business card.

✔    ✔    ✔

I am a woman about to be promoted to an executive position in our firm. Should my card read "Louise Severy," or "Miss Louise Severy?" L.N.Y., New York, New York

It should read "Miss Louise Severy." A woman who is "Mrs." in business should also use this title (Mrs.) on her card, so people may know how to address her.

✔    ✔    ✔

I am a doctor and have both social and business checks. I plan to have them imprinted by the bank. Should my business checks carry my title differently than my social ones? Dr. E.M., Brunswick, New Jersey

Yes. The imprint on your business check should read:

"Edward Moore, M.D."

with the address. On your social checks the name appears as

"Dr. Edward Moore"

with either your business address or home address, depending on how you manage your personal bookkeeping.

## GIFTS

I worked with two girls for eight years, and we became very good friends and exchanged Christmas gifts. Then, three years ago I changed jobs (but we still exchanged gifts), and this year I would like to stop buying gifts for them as I haven't seen them for three years and I want to cut down my Christmas list. I would like to write them a nice letter and tell them so but I can't seem to find the words to do it without hurting their feelings. How do you think this should be handled? V.D., Montreal, Canada

Do it in a simple, direct, and friendly way. Write them well before Christmas and say that, while you have always valued your mutual giving at this season of the year, you find that this year you must cut your Christmas giving to your immediate circle but that you hope that as friends you will always exchange cards and at least once a year give each other news. Undoubtedly they too will be vastly relieved that you have taken the initiative in what is so often an embarrassing situation.

᛫     ᛫     ᛫

My boss gets a lot of presents at various times from firms that supply us. The salesmen's cards are usually enclosed, and I wonder how we should handle the thanks on this. Should we just thank the salesman when he comes around, do I write for the boss, or does the boss dictate a letter? Miss M.E.W., Oakland, California

I think it depends very much on the status of the salesmen in relation to the importance of your boss. Certainly your boss should not take his time to write a personal note to every salesman who sends him a calendar or some other gift advertising services offered. However, you may, verbally, when you see the salesman, thank him if you wish, but in such cases his gift is really a business getter and merely requires passing acknowledgment at your convenience. There are some salesmen who are definitely in the executive class themselves and who give gifts of some importance to major customers. In a case like this your boss should dictate a brief note of thanks, if he himself has personal contact with the salesman. If he never sees him, you yourself could write such a letter of acknowledgment which might begin, "Mr. Brown has asked me to thank you, etc." Where business gifts are exchanged between people who are on a social basis as well, the acknowledgments are always on the social level—often handwritten on personal stationery. However, many executives dictate such letters on special executive stationery, and today this is quite acceptable too.

## TELEPHONE COURTESY

**I am a personal secretary for a major executive of my firm. When my phone rings should I say, "Miss Brown speaking" or should I say, "Mr. Carstair's office, Miss Brown speaking" or just "Mr. Carstair's office." M.J.B., Flemington, New Jersey**

You say "Mr. Carstair's office," and add, if you wish, "Miss Brown speaking."

♪    ♪    ♪

**A new clerk is in the office—not a secretary, just a clerk. Usually answering the phone calls from the outside, she says "Miss Monroe speaking." At times she will put the name of the company first but always manages to put her name in also. As her name wouldn't be of any advantage to the customers, I am curious to know if this is the right or wrong procedure. She is not on the selling end. A.M.F., Bangor, Maine**

Such a clerk should answer "The Jones Company," not "Miss Monroe speaking." As she has no official capacity, presumably the outside world is not interested in her name, and in this instance I can see no reason why she should announce it. On the other hand, if the phone call came in to her desk from the switchboard she would assume that someone wanted to talk to her in particular and would answer, "Miss Monroe speaking"—the proper business procedure.

✓   ✓   ✓

**In calling up a doctor—or someone else whom you are going to consult for a service—is it correct to ask, "How are you?" first, or should you say, "Doctor, this is Mrs. So-and-so, I have a head-ache, etc." A.S.L., Somerville, Massachusetts**

Just announce your name and say immediately what you want. It is best to ask for an appointment or to ask the doctor to come to see you without going into a lengthy discussion of your symptoms over the telephone. Illness is most interesting to those immediately concerned, but a doctor must protect himself emotionally from his patients' troubles in order to best serve them. It's more important to him and to you that he act to relieve your trouble than that he commiserate with you at length. At that, most doctors are reasonably sympathetic. If they didn't have innate sympathy for the troubles of others it is unlikely that they would have become doctors in the first place.

✓   ✓   ✓

**How should an executive (a man) answer his business phone? I was taught it is very impolite for a man to use his own title when referring to himself, except to servants or other employees. Can you set me straight? Mr. H.A.M., Winston-Salem, North Carolina**

In this country, an executive answering his own phone says merely "Hello," or "John Black speaking." He refers to himself as "Mr. Black" to servants and to employees who do not call him by his first name. To his clients or customers, he identifies himself on the phone as "John Black" if they know him well and as "John Black of the Ace Company" if their contact is more casual. If he is calling upon a woman on a business matter, he says, "This is Mr. Black," adding his company's name if needed.

## FAMILIAR PROBLEMS

**Does business etiquette differ from social etiquette in regard to a gentleman's treatment of a lady?** O.L., Moscow, Idaho

Yes, in many cases it does. A subordinate woman employee, for example, usually rises if a top male executive approaches her desk to give her some instruction. She does not do this for her immediate superior, as it would mean she would be jumping up and down all the time. She rises for a superior woman executive too, under the same circumstances—that is, if her desk is visited by a superior with whom she is not in constant contact. She rises too for an important client or customer of the firm to whom she is introduced, whether male or female.

✓ ✓ ✓

**Is it correct for an employer to address his secretary and other women employees by their first names?** M.C.J., Detroit, Michigan

I myself dislike the idea. I think it's a bad thing for an employer to start, because it makes his relationship with his employees too personal. When he must reprimand or discharge someone, it is hard to be objective. It also encourages outsiders to call the office staff, especially the girls, by their first names, which I think is destructive of office dignity.

✓ ✓ ✓

**When taking dictation must the book be placed on the lap of the stenographer, or is it quite proper to use the space on the boss's desk?** L.B.B., Seattle, Washington

It's certainly much more convenient to put it on the desk and probably produces neater notes.

✓ ✓ ✓

**As I am going to continue working after my marriage I thought it would be simpler for me to still use my maiden name. What do you think?** H.S., St. Louis, Missouri

I think it makes things much simpler if a girl who continues to work after her marriage uses her maiden name.

*    *    *

**Recently I saw a salesman come into a store with his hat on and with a cigar in his mouth. He removed neither the hat nor the cigar while talking to the manager of the store. I thought this very rude. Mrs. O.W.H., Roanoke, Virginia**

It was not only rude but poor salesmanship. Anyone, man or woman, should remove anything he is smoking when he speaks to anyone, whether or not he is trying to make a sale. A salesman should also remove his hat in any indoor situation, even when he is trying to make a sale to a man. Anyone in a buying position is quite consciously influenced by deference on the part of the person who is trying to sell him something.

*    *    *

**There is a girl sitting near me in the office who indulges in loud gum-chewing and -snapping all day long. What is your opinion of this? What can I do to stop it? L.D.F., Winthrop, Massachusetts**

Gum-chewing, I feel, is often a good release for tension, but it should certainly be done most privately. Undoubtedly your co-worker is not conscious of the fact that she makes so much noise. If you speak to her yourself she may be offended. The best thing is to take your problem to the office manager, as such things come within her, or his, province.

*    *    *

**In my work I travel quite a lot on trains. Is it ever correct for me to permit a man to buy me a drink, either alcoholic or non-alcoholic, on these trips? Miss W.P., Chicago, Illinois**

No, never permit strangers, especially men, to buy drinks for you on a train or in a terminal. And do not accept any invitations from such strangers for entertainment at the end of the journey, unless you arrange for friends or business acquaintances to join you. This rule applies even to older women traveling for business or social purposes.

✓     ✓     ✓

Recently when I went into a business office and told the receptionist my name, I heard her go to the office of her employer and say, "A Miss Woodward is calling." This seems very rude to me. W.B., Peoria, Illinois

Yes, it was. If you had not given her a card, she should have asked whom you represented. She should then properly have said, "A lady to see you" and handed him your card, or if you had no card, "Miss Woodward calling." If her employer didn't know you he might then ask her to find out, tactfully, why you were calling, or he might have sent out his secretary for the same purpose or to invite you in.

✓     ✓     ✓

Do you think it is good taste for a receptionist to smoke at her desk? Miss A.C.G., Springfield, Illinois

No, I do not. A receptionist should be the most courteous face of the company. She should look pleasant, act pleasant, and be all attention when anyone approaches her desk—even a salesman. She can't be any of these things with a cigarette in her hand. She may, of course, smoke away from her desk in her periods of rest.

✓     ✓     ✓

Would you please give me some information on Christmas gifts to an employer? I am a private secretary to an executive in a large corporation and have received nice gifts from the boss and his wife at Christmas time and on several other occasions. I have often thought of getting him something for his desk, or perhaps something for their teen-age daughter but don't wish to embarrass him. Would a nice plant sent to his home directly from the florist be in good order? J.C., New Hyde Park, New York

No. Do not give them gifts yourself, although you may send a Christmas card, of course. At the executive level, gifts are sometimes exchanged between the boss and his employees, although not

necessarily so. Actually such gifts from an employer are gifts from
the corporation or the company, not gifts from him personally.
They are part of his business expense. Should you have much
social contact with the family, that is, if you are entertained by
them as a friend rather than as an employee, you then, of course,
may give Christmas gifts if you want on a personal basis—not on a
business one.

✓    ✓    ✓

**I am a woman executive and one of my main duties is enter-
taining customers for the firm. When these customers are men
is it permissible for me to pick up the luncheon check as a
representative of my organization?** Mrs. R.K., Chicago, Illinois

Yes, you may, saying something such as "This is business—you're
the firm's guest." If the bill is to be paid at the desk, quietly put
money to cover it on the check and ask your customer to take care
of it. Either leave the tip yourself or ask him to take care of it out
of the change. Try to avoid passing any money yourself, for other
diners in the restaurant would not necessarily understand the circumstances. The most graceful thing to do, of course, is to make
arrangements with the restaurant before you take in a man to
luncheon or dinner. Arrange to sign the check at the desk, use
your credit card, or have monthly bills sent to you at the office if
possible. If you can entertain such customers at your own club
where you may have an account, that is also a good idea. Another
solution is to invite a man from your organization to come along
with you and to ask him to pay the bill. You can either give him
the money for it before leaving or ask him to put in a voucher
if you are sure he has money enough with him to cover the entertainment.

✓    ✓    ✓

The wives of some of our executives here make a habit of drop-
ping in at their husbands' office in the midst of our busiest days.
They use the company's phones, ask their husbands' private secre-
taries to make hairdressing appointments for them. Sometimes
they even park their children with us for an hour or so if they
can get away with that. Mostly, I think the husbands feel about

this the way we girls do, but they don't dare say so. But it might help if you said something about it. Miss L.B., New York, New York

Women who have worked themselves rarely are guilty of this kind of discourtesy. They understand all too well that their husbands work for a corporation and that social encroachments on the corporation's time are actually dishonest. Of course, there are exceptions when an executive's wife might have her husband's secretary do something for her—but the request should always come from the husband. A secretary resents very much being ordered around by her employer's wife. And, as I have said, this takes time away not necessarily from her employer's work, but from the corporation for whom he works. I would say that a wife's visits to a husband's office should be limited in the extreme. And a man even with the most charming children should think twice before having them descend upon the office except on very special occasions, perhaps during the Christmas holidays when he might like to show them off. But he needs to be in a very secure position in order to do even this.

✓    ✓    ✓

I am a TV artist, soon to make my first trip abroad professionally. I have used my maiden name in my career and feel that using my married name on my passport might create some confusion, as I am traveling with a group which does not know me under that name. Is it possible to apply for a passport in my maiden name? Miss W.H.Y., Plainfield, New Jersey

Yes. The Department of State tells me that a married woman who uses her maiden name for professional purposes must submit affidavits of two or more persons to the effect that she has used such a name for professional purposes for a stated period of time.

✓    ✓    ✓

As a married woman how do I register to vote? Mrs. D.B., Millersville, Pennsylvania

You sign it with your legal name, not your social name; that is, "Anne May Smith," not "Mrs. John Smith." There seems to be no objection to your signing it "Anne Clarke (your maiden name) Smith." In most states, I am told, a person may use any name he chooses on legal or other documents so long as there is no intent to defraud. If a married woman prefers to sign herself "Anne Clarke Smith" rather than "Anne May Smith," there is usually no objection, and I myself feel that this is a more distinguishing name than one which uses the first two Christian names—if there are two—with the married name.

✓   ✓   ✓

**Is it correct, in a firm, for the name plates on the partners' inner doors to be shown as "Mr. Jones" or "Mr. Brown," rather than using the full name or initials, such as "John Jones" or "J. Jones and George Brown?"** L.R., Detroit, Michigan

Use "Mr. Jones." And in the case of a woman, you use "Miss Jones" or "Mrs. Brown." If the name is to be put on the door which faces the public hallway, the name of course is then spelled out in full, i.e., "John Jones."

# DIVORCE, SEPARATION, AND WIDOWHOOD

## *Dear Miss Vanderbilt:*

### YOUR CORRECT NAME

Some questions have arisen between myself and some of my friends, more recently widowed, as to present-day designation of widows. Since we belong to the generation that was taught to resume their personal names in place of those of their husbands, we find some questions left unanswered by current etiquette dicta. I gather from what you have written that in addressing this letter to you I should refer to you as "Miss Amy Vanderbilt." But my friends and I are in doubt as to the *correct designation* of the widow of several husbands or of the divorced wife of several husbands. I would appreciate your comments. Mrs. E.S.C., Monterey, California

A widow remains "Mrs. John Smith" in deference to her husband until she remarries. A divorced woman either resumes her maiden name or combines her own surname with her former husband's surname, becoming "Mrs. Jones Smith." Sometimes if she has children by a previous marriage she returns to that husband's surname combining it with her own—"Mrs. Jones Brown"—so she and the children will bear the same name. A professional woman such as myself usually finds it much simpler to use her maiden name throughout her professional career despite marriage.

I was divorced from my husband several years ago and now he is dead. I would like to know how my calling cards should read. Mrs. S.C., Providence, Rhode Island

When you were divorced you no longer could use your husband's first name in connection with his last. You probably followed the correct procedure of appending your maiden name to his name. In other words, you became "Mrs. Smith Green." His recent death has nothing to do with the name that you are to use on your calling cards, since you are not legally his widow but, instead, his divorced wife. Therefore, you use the name "Mrs. Smith Green" on your card. If you were legally his widow you would, of course, have on your card, after his death, the same name you used prior to his death. You would be "Mrs. John Green." It is incorrect for a widow, after her husband's death, to call herself on cards or socially, "Mrs. Mary Green." She retains his name until she remarries.

✦    ✦    ✦

I am a recent divorcée, and I'm not sure whether it is proper for me to wear my wedding ring. I have two children. What do you advise? V.B., Fargo, North Dakota

A divorcée usually removes her wedding ring, even when she has children, and wears her engagement ring on other than the third finger of her left hand. Or she has it redesigned into some other article of jewelry, if indeed she wears it at all.

✦    ✦    ✦

Within the next few months my divorce will be final. I have a choice, I know, of returning to my maiden name or of using a combination of my maiden name and my married name. However, I have children. Would it be preferable for me to use "Mrs.," retaining my married name and preceding it with my former maiden name for the children's sake? E.F.F., Madison, Wisconsin

It is usually simpler that way when there are children. However, there are instances wherein a woman has married twice and has children by the first marriage but not by the second. In this case she sometimes chooses to return to her first married name to simplify matters. She uses it plus her former maiden name. In some rare instances, but also correctly, if for some reason she does not wish to use the name of her former husband or husbands, she returns to her maiden name and for the sake of the children precedes it by "Mrs." rather than "Miss." In order that she not be called "Mrs. Mary" she then must find some surname in her family that will do. If her grandmother's name, for example, was Worthington, she may become "Mrs. Worthington Grant." A mother who has long been in professional life may, if she is divorced, assume for all purposes, legal, social, and professional, her professional name and for simplicity's sake be "Miss" at all times, even when she has children. This is not advisable, however, unless she is so prominent that she is generally identified by everybody with her maiden name.

*      *      *

**I am a new widow with an eighteen-year-old son. Would it be proper for me not to wear my wedding ring? Having had a happily married life, I hope I can have a home again. Also, should I be introduced as "Mrs. Bronson" or as "Catherine Bronson?"** C.B.S., Hot Springs, Colorado

Whether or not you continue to wear your wedding ring is a matter of your own choice. However, you are "Mrs. Bronson"—actually "Mrs. John Bronson"—and not, as a widow, "Mrs. Catherine Bronson," as I feel it necessary to repeat many times.

With very few exceptions, any woman who really puts her mind to marrying can do so. It is only fantasy that a woman must be beautiful, young, talented, physically desirable—to be claimed in the marriage market. A glance around you will show this very clearly. Women—tall, short, old, young, fat, thin, pretty, and ugly —all seem to find husbands. At a time like this I think your friends can be of great help. It is they who spread the word to eligible men whom they invite to their homes, where you will be, that you are available once more. It is easy in conversation to let it be known to any man who interests you that you are a widow. The fact of your previous happy life should make it easy for you to remarry and to make you sought after as a wife.

## YOUR SOCIAL LIFE

I am a widow of forty-five and considered quite attractive. I have several young children but no servants. I live in a small community, and I wonder if it is all right for me to entertain male guests weekends, or will people gossip? R.S.L., Cedar Rapids, Iowa

People will gossip whether or not you have male guests under these circumstances. A woman of forty-five is her own chaperone usually today, and the presence of the children, when your guest is there overnight, should be an additional safeguard. Every woman, however, should value her reputation and conduct herself in such a way that she does not make a public display of her very private life.

✓     ✓     ✓

My young husband died recently under tragic circumstances. I was left with three young children and the need to readjust as quickly as possible to the situation so as to go back to the job I held before marriage. My days are filled with work for the children, but my evenings are understandably lonely. My friends have been very kind, but I wonder what the new convention is about my going out again with men. Am I supposed not to do so for a year as some of my conventional older friends insist? Mrs. M.M.S., Los Angeles, California

Although, as you say, it has been only a few weeks since your husband's death, I feel your own need for social contacts is of more importance than outworn notions of decorum. Today we know that the bereaved must be helped to take their places again in their communities under normal circumstances as quickly as possible. However, in your sensitive state, mourning as of course you are privately, you do not want to subject yourself to the criticism of older people who perhaps do not quite understand how our thinking has changed. If I were you I would accept an occasional invitation from a man to go to the movies or to the theater, to dinner or to the house of friends. I would not go dancing in a public place just yet. It might be better to go out quietly with various escorts rather than to permit the attention of just one. I think that restrained social activity should not be expected of you after about three months from the date of your bereavement. You may then give parties yourself and act as would any young woman of your age under regular social conditions.

✓ ✓ ✓

**My husband is very friendly with his former wife, the mother of his two sons. He visits her to see the children at least once a week and stays to dinner. Do you think I should be invited at this time? He seems to think not. Mrs. W.K.L., Boise, Idaho**

Yes, he is right. He needs to see the children without your presence. Your being there would only remind them of the loss they've had to adjust to and could create considerable tension no matter how fond they may be of you. Under ordinary circumstances it is wisest for their mother not to be present at that time and for their father to have dinner with his children alone. But these things have to be worked out according to individual circumstances so that whatever is done is least painful emotionally.

✓ ✓ ✓

**A couple in our neighborhood has been divorced, but both are living in the area. We have no quarrel with either one of them and would like to extend invitations to them for parties we give throughout the year. Are we supposed to make a choice or may we invite them both, so long as we don't invite them together? Mrs. K.P., Syracuse, New York**

Sometimes when a divorce has been what is called "scandalous," it is difficult for people who have been friends of both couples not to make a social choice when both remain in the community. Sometimes those who were first the friends of the husband continue to see him, and those who were, before the marriage, friends of the wife, continue to see her. Others who knew both equally well sometimes find it necessary to make a choice, but this is only necessary usually when there is bad feeling between the divorced couple. The important thing for friends to remember is not to carry tales from one to the other, if they are entertaining both socially—and, of course, separately. And the divorced people should not ask their friends to give them news of the other or involve their friends in their own personal problems of adjustment. After all, the divorced must make their new ways, socially, and must learn to put the bitter past behind them—especially if they are to be sought-after guests.

✓    ✓    ✓

**Recently I was divorced. My immediate friends, of course, know about it, but I have a wide correspondence. Should I write to my friends explaining what happened or just mention it as the opportunity arises in my regular letters to them?** W.F.A., New Orleans, Louisiana

If close relatives are among those with whom you correspond it is wise to write to them briefly, so that they do not hear the news through others. I feel that people are usually rather embarrassed to have to hear or read the intimate details of such things. Certainly it is not necessary for you to write in any detail. As all divorce is really sad you might write first of other things and then say, "You will be sorry to hear, I know, that Harry and I were divorced a few weeks ago." If there is anything to add about children, for example, you will say, "The children will live with me here and seem to be accepting the situation as well as possible." More than this you certainly need not say in a letter, nor has anyone the right to demand a fuller explanation. You will find in time that you will want to say less and less about the causes of your divorce. And it is well for friends to realize that the true causes of divorce are rarely told and often not really well-known even by the parties involved. A wise man once replied, when asked why he had divorced such a seemingly perfect wife, "Look at the shoes on my feet. Are they not handsome and of fine quality? And yet, which of you can tell me where they pinch me?"

✓    ✓    ✓

**I have been keeping company with a man for ten years. My brother, with whom I lived, died a few weeks ago. How long should I wait before getting married?** C.G.A., Medford, Massachusetts

It depends very much on the community in which you live and the circumstances. I assume that you must have taken care of your brother, relinquishing marriage yourself. I feel that it is only fair for you to marry as soon as you wish, but if you want to be really proper you could wait three months from the time of his death, which is more or less the modern idea of mourning. Why not discuss this with your friends—people who mean much to you—and see how they feel about it? I am sure that many would urge you to marry now as you have certainly done your duty and it would seem unfair to keep your fiancé waiting longer. I would urge, however, a quiet ceremony rather than a formal wedding.

ℐ ℐ ℐ

**I am a widow of four months and have started going out with a nice man. He wants to get married but my family thinks I should wait a year to show respect for my deceased husband. I am forty. Would it be disrespectful for me to marry now?** Mrs. E.R.J., Topeka, Kansas

Such things depend very much on community custom. In your case, if you had known the man prior to your widowhood and there would be no possibility of gossip concerning you both, I think you might marry in the sixth month of your widowhood. Why not discuss this with your friends and your clergyman and see how they feel about it? Generally the old rule of waiting a year is good for a reason we usually don't think of. A year gives time for the wounds of grief to heal. At four months you may feel so greatly deprived of your husband that this new man seems to be literally heaven-sent. After a year of friendship and courtship you may feel differently. You may find, also, that there are other men interested in you and that you will have a choice. It is not necessary to feel panicky at forty anymore about the possibility of another husband. Be sure that it isn't this that makes you think you are in love and ready to marry again so soon.

# DRESS

## *Dear Miss Vanderbilt:*

### BUSINESS

Do you think it's all right for a junior executive to wear slacks
and a sports jacket to his office, especially when the senior executives do so? H.R., Denver, Colorado

The production of men's slacks is up by millions of pairs, so not
only are men wearing more slacks with odd jackets but may be
expected to wear more of them in the future. The young employee, however, is expected to wear a complete suit in the more
conservative organizations. Young executives may wear slacks and
odd jackets, especially in the summertime if others in their group
do so. A man who works out of his office in the country, or a man
actually working in the country, such as a suburban doctor, may
certainly wear them.

⚹ ⚹ ⚹

What type of clothing do you consider most suitable for a secretary to wear to work? G.H., La Jolla, California

It depends on the community in which she works. If she works in
a large city, she wears tailored, conservative clothes, low or me-
dium, not high, heels, stockings (even in the hottest weather),
minimum of jewelry and none of it clanking, conservative make-up
and nails, and a simple coiffure. If she works under country conditions, she wears simple country clothes, which again should be
on the conservative side. In the country, for example, sweaters

and skirts worn with or without jackets are acceptable, but sweaters in a city are often not permitted.

✓   ✓   ✓

Maybe you can help me. I am a single man just making my way in my profession. Shall I buy expensive shoes at $25.00 and up—if I can afford only a few pairs—or shall I buy inexpensive but neat looking shoes and use my budget money for better suits, hats, and top coats? Other men I know say that it pays to buy an expensive suit and shoes, if only a couple, rather than several suits and several pairs of shoes that are not expensive. What is your view on the situation? K.H., Chicago, Illinois

My grandfather used to say that he judged a man by his shoes. Certainly shabby shoes, or ones that lose their shape and crack easily, can spoil the entire impression of a man's wardrobe. I agree with your friend that you should buy the most expensive shoes that you can in relation to your over-all budget. Inexpensive shoes lose their shape and wear out so quickly that in the end they are really no saving. Two good pairs of shoes, brown and black, with an inexpensive pair of summer shoes, should take you through the year and maybe much longer. If you watch the sales you should buy those $25 shoes for $12 or $15, you know.

## PARTIES AND OTHER SOCIAL OCCASIONS*

What is the proper attire for a cocktail party from five to eight for the hostess and for the guests? Mrs. A.H., Beloit, Wisconsin

The hostess wears a short or long cocktail dress or hostess pajamas suitable to the time of the year. The women guests wear fairly dressy clothes such as silk suits, black or jewel-colored cocktail dresses, cottons, linens, or wools (depending on the season) with or without hats. The men wear dark suits in the winter, linen or any of the tropical weaves in the summer or, in the country, sports jackets and odd trousers. It is the rare cocktail

---

* The subject of Dress is also discussed in the Engagements and Weddings, Funerals, and Your Manners Away from Home sections.

party today that is important and formal enough, in the city, to turn out the cutaways or director's jackets, but if in doubt, ask the hostess.

✓  ✓  ✓

**At a cocktail party is it correct for ladies to remove their hats? A.R.H., New Haven, Connecticut**

If they wish. And of course they may even come without hats if that's their preference.

✓  ✓  ✓

**Recently several couples who were staying at the same hotel during a convention were invited to dinner in the hotel dining room. With one exception, we women wore dressy, street-length dresses and no hats. One of us wore a severe suit and a hat. The dinner was at eight o'clock in the main dining room. The rest of us felt that the suited one did not display good taste. We'd appreciate your opinion. H.G.S., Trenton, New Jersey**

As you were all attending a convention, perhaps she was unable to change in time, as you were. You were, of course, more appropriately dressed as, in this instance, the hotel dining room is treated as your own home under party circumstances. If it was necessary for your friend to dress in her business clothes she should have made a brief, unembarrassed apology.

✓  ✓  ✓

**When women dress formally, shouldn't men follow suit? F.L.A., Peoria, Illinois**

Our growing informality has placed women, sometimes, in an awkward position in regard to their clothes. Many times I have been in a smart restaurant and seen a woman dressed in dinner clothes, followed by an escort in a sports jacket and sometimes with his hands in his pockets (probably out of sheer embarrassment). Where a man can't or won't dress for an occasion it is bad taste for the woman whom he escorts to be dressed to the hilt, and while I feel a certain informality in entertaining tends to relax us all, it shouldn't relax us so much that we become completely graceless.

✓ ✓ ✓

In going down a receiving line, should ladies remove their gloves?
G.B., Chicago, Illinois

No, not unless they are being introduced to the President of the United States or to royalty which has made such a request (that ladies remove their gloves) to those attending them. A lady would also remove her gloves for a very high church dignitary on a par with the President in position. I would like to note here that it is a rather masculine gesture for a woman to strip off her gloves to shake hands with anyone. Even when she is shaking hands with a woman who is ungloved she does not remove her gloves.

## ACCESSORIES

I am confused as to when to wear a hat and gloves. Many of us here in the Midwest are averse to wearing either, except for comfort. Some of us have one pair of gloves and one hat for each season. But I know there are times when we should wear either or both. Could you give me a few basic rules for life here in the Midwest? Also, does one have to wear white gloves all summer? It seems there are local customs that are accepted etiquette on these things, but where does one go to understand them? Usually I have followed the trial-and-error way and have had embarrassing times. Mrs. J.A.F., Monroe City, Missouri

When in doubt, wear a hat—and gloves. If you arrive at any gathering and find everyone hatless, you may always remove your hat. In very hot weather, in climates such as you have, gloves can certainly be very uncomfortable. Most women carry them, but again it is better to have them and carry them than not to have them with you at all. In New York I prefer to wear white gloves, even on the hottest day, rather than to get my hands full of the grit of the city, and I wouldn't feel myself well-dressed without having them with me.

Here are some simple rules concerning the wearing of a hat and the carrying or wearing of gloves, in most ordinary circumstances:

1. Wear a hat and gloves to church and to any religious ceremony, even one taking place in a home.

2. Wear a hat, or a substitute bow or veil, at any formal reception when you are in daytime dress.

3. Wear a hat when making a formal call on an important person, such as a governor or a bishop.

4. Wear a hat—or be prepared to do so—if you are a featured speaker before any group. This rule is much more rigid in small towns than in big cities where hats are worn, under all circumstances, only if desired (except at funerals, in church, and on very formal occasions). But gloves, even when hats are not worn, are always a must when one is dressed to go out to any place where there is a degree of formality even though they may be carried rather than worn. They should be worn when one goes down the receiving line at a daytime reception of any kind, unless one is being received by the President or by royalty when glovelessness is requested.

✓  ✓  ✓

**When a man is wearing a suit with a vest is it proper for him, when taking off his suit coat to also remove his vest, or should he leave the vest on?** Mrs. C.L., Atlanta, Georgia

Since, in most cases, vests are not made of the same fabric all around, a vest should be removed when the jacket is removed. Of course, jackets should not be taken off unless permission is given.

✓  ✓  ✓

**Is it ever correct for a man to go without garters?** Mrs. R.V., Charleston, South Carolina

The matter of garters for gentlemen is a very touchy question. Of course, it is neater for them to wear garters, especially for business and social occasions, but the fact is that many do not. Some men who are quite fastidious in their dress get around the sloppiness of socks without garters by wearing wool socks which seem to stay in place. They wear them winter and summer. Nylon, rayon, and silk socks, unless they have elastic tops, do seem to require the support of garters if a man is to look well-groomed.

✓      ✓      ✓

**My wife says that it is incorrect to wear black shoes in the country. What do you think? J.A., New York, New York**

Well, it depends. The choir boy would wear black shoes even in the country church, and black shoes are for formal attire anywhere—for example, cutaways or director's jackets are often worn at formal country events and are of course accompanied by black shoes. But certainly brown shoes are outdoor shoes in the country. And yet the current fashion does show black loafers and even quite a lot of black in country tweeds, so this season at least, and maybe for a few seasons to come, we might abridge the rule, and the kind of black informal shoe I have described would be all right in the country.

✓      ✓      ✓

**Is it really good taste to wear the cross as jewelry, as I see so many girls doing? M.O.K., Toledo, Ohio**

Yes, it is in good taste for Christians who try sincerely to epitomize the Christian virtues. Worn this way, however, it is always a plain cross and never a crucifix.

✓      ✓      ✓

**My girl objects to my wearing a diamond ring it took me a long time to save for. She says it's in bad taste for men to wear diamonds. Do you agree? C.J.H., Kansas City, Kansas**

Yes, in this day and age, with the possible exception of small diamond chips in cuff links, diamonds have become very feminine and are considered ostentatious on men. Because men bestow diamonds on women, it is not considered ostentatious for a woman to wear them—if she has them. If a man wears a big diamond he is presumed to have bought it for himself to wear as a beacon of his success—and, practically, as a form of easily negotiable wealth.

✓      ✓      ✓

Is it ever proper to wear an oxford shoe with a moderately dressy afternoon dress? Mrs. A.S.N., Denver, Colorado

Well, it isn't fashionable, but many women with foot trouble, it seems, have no choice, as their doctors insist that they have this kind of support over the instep. However, there are dressy oxfords in suede, and many special manufacturers make shoes with firm support that look better than the oxford with dressy clothes. A woman whose feet hurt can't enjoy herself socially, so their comfort should be a major consideration in her social life.

## SPORTS

In recent years bowling has become a very popular sport for women as well as men. A group of women in our community has formed a bowling league, and now the problem of correct attire at the bowling lanes has come up. We would appreciate your opinion. Mrs. J.B., East Meadow, New York

For bowling, with some of the unflattering positions one must assume, I recommend full skirts, or well-tailored slacks or culottes (below the knees). Straight skirts should be avoided, as they inhibit movement.

✓    ✓    ✓

My daughter is going to start riding lessons. What can I tell her about the proper choice of a riding habit and what to wear with it? I don't want her to be laughed at, and as I've never ridden myself I don't actually know what's right. W.A.J., Kansas City, Missouri

Just tell her that she should avoid fussy feminine riding clothes. Actually, women's riding clothes are adapted from men's fine English habits. They are best in various men's wear—tweed, gabardine, whipcord, linen, etc. Jodhpurs when they are worn should be worn by the quite slender and should fit properly. Jackets are always man-tailored and in conservative woodsy colors either matching or contrasting with the trousers. She should never wear anything such as lapel jewelry with a riding jacket, although a small boutonniere such as a man might wear is acceptable. If the hair is short or can be done in such a way as to keep out of the rider's eyes a hat is not necessary. A hat, when worn, is usually a soft sport felt hat with an unbound brim, again in soft woodsy colors. The shirt worn with a country riding habit is usually white and may be open at the neck or worn with a suitable tie.

**What do you consider proper wear for a woman on the golf course?** L.E.L., Scarsdale, New York

In warm weather, the classic dress for golf is the cotton, flannel, gabardine, or linen shirtwaist golf dress loosely cut for swing action, pleated at the waist in back, and fastening down the front. The neckline is that of a regular shirt, and the belt is usually built in. A golf dress is usually in white, pastel, or neutral shades and is worn with traditional golf shoes with rubber soles or cleats to prevent slipping. The rubber-soled saddle oxford (but only in brown and white) is suitable, as is any sturdy brown leather walking shoe. No heel- and toeless play shoes or aboriginal sandals, please. Bermuda shorts or culottes are also worn now, but many courses frown on skinny pants.

In cold weather, a loose pull-over sweater worn with a shirt, and a comfortably cut wool or flannel skirt is best. A loose tweed jacket or a windbreaker may be worn on top, if you choose to play when it's that cold. Brown leather gloves or the doeskin golf gloves with reinforced palms may be more comfortable than bare hands. Good English lisle hose may replace the usual anklets or be worn with them. Thin wool stockings are a good idea. The reliable, soft round felt in a neutral color or brown is helpful on a windy day.

**I am a married woman in my late thirties. I have a pretty good figure, and I would like to buy a bikini bathing suit. My husband objects, saying that only young girls should wear such revealing suits. I disagree. What is your opinion.** Mrs. C.S., Long Beach, California

I agree with your husband. Be absolutely sure of your pretty good figure. I feel that bikini bathing suits are only for the very young —and the slim ones at that.

✓   ✓   ✓

I am on the heavy side and wonder what would be the best kind of bathing suit for me to wear—I mean fabric and cut and color. Mrs. J.L.M., Los Angeles, California

So-called dressmaker suits are best for you—a tailored suit with a brief skirt that covers your thighs gracefully. Avoid midriff suits and those in shiny materials. Many of the new suits have built-in —or woven-in—features that improve the figure considerably. Black, navy, brown, dark green, dark gray all make you seem slimmer than the vivid colors. Get an early and thorough tan if you can manage it, and this too will seem to make you slimmer.

## RELIGIOUS SERVICES

Will you please say whether it is proper for men to go to church without wearing their coats and to communion in shirt sleeves? My nephew and quite a few men go to church and communion in their shirt sleeves. I told him he should not go up to the altar without his coat. Mrs. J.C., Waco, Texas

Yes. I must agree with you. On the Sabbath, and especially for communion, a man should approach the altar in coat and tie. He may come and go to the church in his shirt sleeves if that is the custom of his group and the weather is intolerable, but certainly he must maintain the utmost dignity in church.

✓   ✓   ✓

I occasionally visit churches other than my own when visiting friends. What is the etiquette regarding proper dress in the different places of worship? Mrs. J.P., Jacksonville, Florida

We wear conservative "best" clothes, and we tastefully refrain from wearing extreme hats or bright clothes that would seem to distract the other worshipers from their meditations. In the Roman Catholic church and Orthodox synagogues, hats for women are required. In Protestant Episcopal churches, Conservative and Reform synagogues, hats for women are requested. In many other denominations women usually do wear hats to church on the Sabbath, as well as gloves. Churches throughout the country are open for prayer and meditation during the week, however, and this raises the question as to whether or not one must hesitate to enter a church in working clothes. Of course one need not. The door is open to invite anyone who wishes to enter for spiritual refreshment. However, the hat convention can be followed very simply by a woman even when she has no hat with her. She merely covers her head when she enters with a handkerchief or scarf and leaves it in place until she goes out.

✓ ✓ ✓

**I was taught as a little girl that one must never cross one's legs in church or wear a lot of perfume. Yet I find many people ignoring both of these customs or whatever you call them. Mrs. J.F.S., Glen Cove, New York**

Neither of these is a matter of church regulations. We are so used now to sitting with our legs crossed that the Victorian edict of having a lady's feet strictly on the floor at church and for social occasions is no longer valid. Plenty of perfectly nice people cross their legs in church. However, heavy perfume is certainly not a good idea, for it draws attention to a single worshiper and possibly distracts those around her.

# INDEX

I

SEP 26 '67